SELECTED POEMS

SELECTED POEMS

ROBERT CREELEY

UNIVERSITY OF CALIFORNIA PRESS

Berkeley • Los Angeles • London

This selection first published in 1991 by
Marion Boyars Publishers Ltd
24 Lacy Road, London SW15 INL

Grateful acknowledgment is made to the original
publishers of the books from which other
poems in this volume have been reprinted: *Thirty
Things* (Santa Barbara, Calif.: Black Sparrow, 1974),
Backwards (Knotting, Bedfordshire: Sceptre, 1975),
Away (Santa Barbara, Calif.: Black Sparrow, 1976),
and *It: Francesco Clemente/64 Pastels, Robert Creeley/
12 Poems* (Zurich: Edition Gallery Bruno
Bischofberger, 1989).

Library of Congress Cataloging-in-Publication Data

Creeley, Robert, 1926–
[Poems. Selections]
Selected poems / Robert Creeley.
p. cm.
"A Centennial book"—P.
Includes index.
ISBN 0-520-06935-8 (cloth)
ISBN 0-520-06936-6 (pbk.: alk. paper)
I. Title.
PS3505.R43A6   1991   91-7152
811'.54—dc20   CIP

Printed in the United States of America

08   07   06   05   04   03
9   8   7   6   5

for my sister
Helen

CONTENTS

PREFACE

The prospect of this book argued that much might be qualified and recollected, so that it all might be a fact of retrospective clarity, but nonetheless a legitimate one—or so I felt. But now I think of very little other than what's always been obvious to the readers of my work, the company I've kept and the insistent necessity to "get said," in William Carlos Williams' phrase, "what must be said . . ." Just how it was I otherwise began to make poems I have now no recollection except that words in themselves were early a delight and value to me. In poetry they were, as Pound said, most fully charged with meaning.

It was also Ezra Pound who first impressed me with his emphasis, "Only emotion endures." Just a few nights ago I heard a friend from college days, talking about artificial intelligence, his authority. He noted the banality, in some respects, of emotions, that is, how, neurologically, they are a familiar spectrum and shift almost crudely from one to another—whereas the intellectual acts which are so sponsored, what we *think* thus funded, are of extreme human interest and consequence. Again Williams: "The poet thinks with his poem, in that lies his thought, and that in itself is the profundity." No doubt it is all a dream, humanly speaking, but how language thinks to say it, what it thus makes of its own mind and feeling, is to me forever provocative. "A new world is only a new mind, and the poem and the mind are all apiece."

I had wanted, in fact, to write prose, novels, as I imagined, which might support myself and family in a modest but specific manner. I'm sure I had read that into what little I then knew of writers of the time just previous, particularly the twenties with all its American and English heroes. A few stories and an occasional novel would serve us well indeed. Nothing of the sort ever happened, and by the time I was thirty, I'd contrived to teach as a means of living, which I've done ever since. Poetry, which I more and more wrote and also more and more paid allegiance to, could not hold us all together in the common need.

Probably that tentativeness, on my part, to trust entirely to poetry for our wherewithal, was what provoked Robert Graves all those years ago to call me a "domestic poet," and my muse therefore a domestic drudge within that proposedly small world. However, no one who has ever so lived would feel it so, that is, a scrunched limit of possibilities. With Robert Duncan I am committed to the hearth, and love the echoes of that word. The fire is the center.

Paradoxically I've moved endlessly and only now begin to find a place to return to. Possibly the whole world is just that and one cannot be simply partial. Too, the bards were those travellers from one common place to another, bringing the insistent news of how it was elsewhere, inside or out. Finally, the world is round.

Why poetry? Its materials are so constant, simple, elusive, specific. It costs so little and so much. It preoccupies a life, yet can only find one in living. It is a music, a playful construct of feeling, a last word and communion. I love it that these words, "made solely of air," as Williams said, have no owner finally to determine them. The English teacher all that time ago who said, "You must learn to speak correctly," was only wrong in forgetting to say why—for these words which depend upon us for their very existence fail as our usage derides or excludes them. They are no more right or wrong than we are, yet suffer our presumption forever.

The choice of poems here is entirely my own and was quickly resolved. What had stayed in mind was the active measure, no matter why. It would be my dream to return to words entirely, much as Louis Zukofsky does at the end of "A" 23. But now the lessons are over. My thanks to the friends of this life, Pound, Williams, Zukofsky, Olson, Levertov, Duncan, Dorn, Wieners, Mc-

Clure, Ginsberg, and many, many more. Thanks also to Robert Grenier, whose earlier selection of poems for a like occasion (Scribner's, 1976) gave this one a useful confidence. As he'd well know, the rest is silence.

ROBERT CREELEY

Waldoboro, Maine
August 14, 1989

Selected Poems

Return

Quiet as is proper for such places;
The street, subdued, half-snow, half-rain,
Endless, but ending in the darkened doors.
Inside, they who will be there always,
Quiet as is proper for such people—
Enough for now to be here, and
To know my door is one of these.

Still Life Or

mobiles:
         that the wind can catch at,
against itself,
           a leaf or a contrivance of wires,
in the stairwell,
to be looked at from below.

We have arranged the form of a formula here,
have taken the heart out
               & the wind
is vague emotion.

To count on these aspirants
these contenders for the to-be-looked-at part
of these actions
            these most hopeful movements
needs
a strong & constant wind.
                That will not rise
                 ⤷ above the speed
which we have calculated,
              that the leaf
remain
        that the wires
be not too much shaken.

Guido, i' vorrei che
tu e Lapo ed io

Guido,
I would that you, me & Lapo

                      (so a song sung:
                      sempre d'amore . . .)

were out of this
           had got to the reaches
of some other wood.

Deadness
        is echo
deadness is memory
              & their deadness is
petulant, the song gone
dead in their heads.

Echo
      is memory
and all that they foster
                 is dead in its sound
has no ripeness
could come to its own.

Petulance
        is force so contested.
They have twisted
              the meanings & manner
the force of us out of us
left us the faded
           (Who made musick
the sound of the reaches
              the actual wood

Love

Not enough. The question: what is.
Given: grace
                        the time of this moment
which I do not see as time.
The particulars: oak, the grain of, oak.
And what supple shadows may come
to be here.

Tell me something I don't know.
Of love, and I hear it, say:
speak to me, of love . . .
                                 The crouched hand.
The indefatigable.
                         But quicken, but be
the quick!

. . . *the stain of love is upon the world!*

Which I have not written.

Something for Easter

I pulled the street up as you suggested
—and found what?
                          1 nickel
                          2 pieces gum
etc.

But we are practical
—but winter is long & however much one
does save, there is never
enough.

A Poem

If the water forms
the forms of the weeds, there—

a long life is not by that
a necessarily happy one.

My friend. We
reckon on a simple

agreement,
the fashion of a stone

underground.

Old Song

Take off your clothes, love,
And come to me.

Soon will the sun be breaking
Over yon sea.

And all of our hairs be white, love,
For aught we do

And all our nights be one, love,
For all we knew.

The Charm

My children are, to me,
what is uncommon: they are dumb
and speak with signs. Their hands

are nervous, and fit more for
hysteria, than goodwill or long
winterside conversation.

Where fire is, they are quieter
and sit, comforted. They were born
by their mother in hopelessness.

But in them I had been, at first,
tongue. If they speak,
I have myself, and love them.

The Pedigree

Or if I will not rape
my own daughter
                    "What will I do?"

What, of what occasion, is not so
necessary, we do not
                    "witless"
perform it.

            Or me.
Who am of common stock.

The Europeans

Or me wanting another man's
wife, etc.

        History.

Unable to keep straight
generations.

Telling them all about
myself.

Eros

Also the headache of
to do right by feeling
it don't matter, etc.

But otherwise it was one, or even two
the space of, felt

and one night I said to her, do you
and she didn't.

The Revelation

I thought that if I were broken enough
I would see the light
like at the end of a small tube, but approachable.

I thought chickens laid eggs
for a purpose.

For the reason expected, a form occurred more
blatant and impossible

to stop me.

An Obscene Poem

The girl in the bikini, my
wife, the lady—she sits on
the rocks, crouched
behind a jagged encumbrance.

Calamares, canalones—
the fisherman's daughter.
At night a dull movement
on the sands

and lightly at low tide
on the rocks
bland, undulant
she returns.

Chasing the Bird

The sun sets unevenly and the people
go to bed.

The night has a thousand eyes.
The clouds are low, overhead.

Every night it is a little bit
more difficult, a little

harder. My mind
to me a mangle is.

Hi There!

Look, love
            * * * * * *
                (oo)
                        springs
from out the
            * * * * * *
                (oo)
                ( )
                        surface of a pedestrian
fact, a new
            * * * * * *
                (oo)
                ( )
                (----)
                    day.

The Happy Man

Who would love you
if you were not six

feet tall, a ruddy face, a
smiling face. You

would walk all night, all
night, and no one, no one

would look at you.

For Somebody's Marriage

All night in a thoughtful
mood, she

resigned herself to a
conclusion—heretofore

rejected. She
woke lonely,

she had
slept well, yet

because of it her
mind was clearer, less

defended—
though confident.

Stomping with Catullus

1

My love—my love says
she loves me.
And that she would never have
anyone but me.

Though what a woman tells
to a man who pushes her
should be written in wind and quickly
moving water.

2

My old lady says I'm it,
she says nobody else cd ever make it.

But what my old lady says when pushed to it,—
well, that don't make it.

3

My old lady is a goof at heart,
she tells me she loves me, we'll never part—

but what a goofed up chick will tell to a man
is best written in wind & water & sand.

4

Love & money & a barrel of mud,
my old man gives out for stud,

comes home late from his life of sin,
now what do you think I should tell to him?

5

We get crazy but we have fun,
life is short & life gets done,

time is now & that's the gig,
make it, don't just flip yr wig.

For a Friend

You are the one man
coming down the street on

a bicycle. And love is a certainty
because it is sure of itself.

The alphabet is letters,
the muskrat was a childhood friend.

But love is eternal,
and pathetic equally.

"To Work Is to Contradict Contradictions, to Do Violence to Natural Violence . . ."

To consummate
the inconsummate, and make of it

the unending. Work,
work, work.

Six days of the week you shall work,
on the seventh you shall think about it.

'Mary, pass the potatoes' becomes
division of subject & object.

Work, work, work.
Get them yourself.

Thought is a process of work,
joy is an issue of work.

The Picnic

for Ed and Helene

Ducks in the pond,
ice cream & beer,
all remind me
of West Acton, Mass—

where I lived when young
in a large old house
with 14 rooms
and woods out back.

Last night I talked
to a friend & his wife
about loons & wildcats
and how to live on so much money per month.

Time we all went home,
or back,
to where it all was,
where it all was.

The Passage

What waiting in the halls,
stamping on the stairs,
all the ghosts are here tonight
come from everywhere.

Yet one or two,
absent, make
themselves felt by that,
break the heart.

Oh did you know I love you?
Could you guess?
Do you have, for me,
any tenderness left?

I cry to hear them,
sad, sad voices.
Ladies and gentlemen
come and come again.

The Sentence

There is that in love
which, by the syntax of,
men find women and join
their bodies to their minds

—which wants so to acquire
a continuity, a place,
a demonstration that it must
be one's own sentence.

The Skeleton

The element in which they live,
the shell going outward until
it never can end, formless,
seen on a clear night as stars,
the term of life given them
to come back to, down to,
and then to be in
themselves only, only skin.

The Lion and the Dog

Let who will think of what they will.
If the mind is made up, like an animal,
a lion to be suffered, a dog to pat,
action follows without conclusion

till all is stopped. The conclusion
is not variable, it is. From that
which was, then it, the lion if it is,
or dog, if it is, is not. It has

died to who thought of it, but comes
again there, to wherever that mind was,
or place, or circumstance being compound
of place, and time, now waiting but patient.

And all that is difficult, but difficult
not to think of, saying, lion, dog, thinking,
thinking patience, as an occasion of these,
but never having known them. But they come,

just as they came once, he thought, he
gave them each all that they were, lion,
but a word merely, and only a dog of sound.
All die equally. The mind is only there,

but here he is, thinking of them. They
are patient. What do they know? They know
nothing. They are not but as he thought.
But he knows nothing who thinks. They are.

Hart Crane

for Slater Brown

1

He had been stuttering, by the edge
of the street, one foot still
on the sidewalk, and the other
in the gutter . . .

like a bird, say, wired to flight, the
wings, pinned to their motion, stuffed.

The words, several, and for each, several
senses.
            "It is very difficult to sum up
briefly . . ."
                        It always was.

(Slater, let me come home.
The letters have proved insufficient.
The mind cannot hang to them as it could
to the words.

There are ways beyond
what I have here to work with,
what my head cannot push to any kind
of conclusion.

But my own ineptness
cannot bring them to hand,
the particulars of those times
we had talked.)

"Men kill themselves because they are
afraid of death, he says . . ."

The push
                    beyond and
into

2

Respect, they said he respected the
ones with the learning, lacking it
himself
            (Waldo Frank & his
6 languages)
                    What had seemed
important
While Crane sailed to Mexico I was writing
(so that one betrayed
                            himself)
He slowed
            (without those friends to keep going, to
keep up), stopped
                    dead and the head could not

go further

       without those friends

. . . *And so it was I entered the broken world*

Hart Crane.

      Hart

Le Fou

for Charles

who plots, then, the lines
talking, taking, always the beat from
the breath
        (moving slowly at first
the breath
        which is slow—

I mean, graces come slowly,
it is that way.

So slowly (they are waving
we are moving
        away from (the trees
          the usual (go by
which is slower than this, is
        (we are moving!
goodbye

The Innocence

Looking to the sea, it is a line
of unbroken mountains.

It is the sky.
It is the ground. There
we live, on it.

It is a mist
now tangent to another
quiet. Here the leaves
come, there
is the rock in evidence

or evidence.
What I come to do
is partial, partially kept.

After Lorca

for M. Marti

The church is a business, and the rich
are the business men.
                    When they pull on the bells, the
poor come piling in and when a poor man dies,
⤷ he has a wooden
cross, and they rush through the ceremony.

But when a rich man dies, they
drag out the Sacrament
and a golden Cross, and go *doucement, doucement*
to the cemetery.

And the poor love it
and think it's crazy.

The Dishonest Mailmen

They are taking all my letters, and they
put them into a fire.

                           I see the flames, etc.
But do not care, etc.

They burn everything I have, or what little
I have. I don't care, etc.

The poem supreme, addressed to
emptiness—this is the courage

necessary. This is something
quite different.

The Immoral Proposition

If you never do anything for anyone else
you are spared the tragedy of human relation-

ships. If quietly and like another time
there is the passage of an unexpected thing:

to look at it is more
than it was. God knows

nothing is competent nothing is
all there is. The unsure

egoist is not
good for himself.

For W.C.W.

The pleasure of the wit sustains
a vague aroma

The fox-glove (unseen) the
wild flower

To the hands come
many things. In time of trouble

a wild exultation.

Chanson

Oh, le petit rondelay!
Gently, gently.
It is that I grow older.

As when for a lark
gaily, one hoists up a window
shut many years.

Does the lady's eye grow moist-
er, is it madame's in-
clination,

etc. Oh, le petit rondelay!
Gently, gently.
It is that I grow older.

The Conspiracy

You send me your poems,
I'll send you mine.

Things tend to awaken
even through random communication.

Let us suddenly
proclaim spring. And jeer

at the others,
all the others.

I will send a picture too
if you will send me one of you.

I Know a Man

As I sd to my
friend, because I am
always talking,—John, I

sd, which was not his
name, the darkness sur-
rounds us, what

can we do against
it, or else, shall we &
why not, buy a goddamn big car,

drive, he sd, for
christ's sake, look
out where yr going.

Wait for Me

. . . give a man his
I said to her,

manliness: provide
what you want I

creature comfort
want only

for him and herself:
more so. You

preserve essential
think marriage is

hypocrisies—
everything?

in short, make a
Oh well,

home for herself.
I said.

The Disappointment

Had you the eyes of a goat,
they would be almond, half-green, half-

yellow, an almond
shape to them. Were you

less as you are, cat-like, a brush
head, sad, sad, un-

goatlike.

The Warning

For love—I would
split open your head and put
a candle in
behind the eyes.

Love is dead in us
if we forget
the virtues of an amulet
and quick surprise.

Like They Say

Underneath the tree on some
soft grass I sat, I

watched two happy
woodpeckers be dis-

turbed by my presence. And
why not, I thought to

myself, why
not.

The Whip

I spent a night turning in bed,
my love was a feather, a flat

sleeping thing. She was
very white

and quiet, and above us on
the roof, there was another woman I

also loved, had
addressed myself to in

a fit she
returned. That

encompasses it. But now I was
lonely, I yelled,

but what is that? Ugh,
she said, beside me, she put

her hand on
my back, for which act

I think to say this
wrongly.

Juggler's Thought

for my son, David

Heads up to the sky
people are walking by

in the land with no heads
tails hanging to trees

where truth is like an apple
reddened by frost and sun, and the green

fields go out and out
under the sun.

A Form of Women

I have come far enough
from where I was not before
to have seen the things
looking in at me through the open door

and have walked tonight
by myself
to see the moonlight
and see it as trees

and shapes more fearful
because I feared
what I did not know
but have wanted to know.

My face is my own, I thought.
But you have seen it
turn into a thousand years.
I watched you cry.

I could not touch you.
I wanted very much to
touch you
but could not.

If it is dark
when this is given to you,
have care for its content
when the moon shines.

My face is my own.
My hands are my own.
My mouth is my own
but I am not.

Moon, moon,
when you leave me alone
all the darkness is
an utter blackness,

a pit of fear,
a stench,
hands unreasonable
never to touch.

But I love you.
Do you love me.
What to say
when you see me.

Please

for James Broughton

Oh god, let's go.
This is a poem for Kenneth Patchen.
Everywhere they are shooting people.
People people people people.
This is a poem for Allen Ginsberg.
I want to be elsewhere, elsewhere.
This is a poem about a horse that got tired.
Poor. Old. Tired. Horse.
I want to go home.
I want you to go home.
This is a poem which tells the story,
which is the story.
I don't know. I get lost.
If only they would stand still and let me.
Are you happy, sad, not happy, please come.
This is a poem for everyone.

Oh No

If you wander far enough
you will come to it
and when you get there
they will give you a place to sit

for yourself only, in a nice chair,
and all your friends will be there
with smiles on their faces
and they will likewise all have places.

Goodbye

She stood at the window. There was
a sound, a light.
She stood at the window. A face.

Was it that she was looking for,
he thought. Was it that
she was looking for. He said,

turn from it, turn
from it. The pain is
not unpainful. Turn from it.

The act of her anger, of
the anger she felt then,
not turning to him.

A Wicker Basket

Comes the time when it's later
and onto your table the headwaiter
puts the bill, and very soon after
rings out the sound of lively laughter—

Picking up change, hands like a walrus,
and a face like a barndoor's,
and a head without any apparent size,
nothing but two eyes—

So that's you, man,
or me. I make it as I can,
I pick up, I go
faster than they know—

Out the door, the street like a night,
any night, and no one in sight,
but then, well, there she is,
old friend Liz—

And she opens the door of her cadillac,
I step in back,
and we're gone.
She turns me on—

There are very huge stars, man, in the sky,
and from somewhere very far off someone hands
↳ me a slice of apple pie,
with a gob of white, white ice cream on top of it,
and I eat it—

Slowly. And while certainly
they are laughing at me, and all around me is racket
of these cats not making it, I make it

in my wicker basket.

Air: "Cat Bird Singing"

Cat bird singing
makes music like sounds coming

at night. The trees, goddamn them,
are huge eyes. They

watch, certainly, what
else should they do? My love

is a person of rare refinement,
and when she speaks,

there is another air,
melody—what Campion spoke of

with his
follow thy fair sunne unhappie shadow . . .

Catbird, catbird.
O lady hear me. I have no

other
voice left.

The Traveller

Into the forest again
whence all roads depend
this way and that
to lead him back.

Upon his shoulders
he places boulders,
upon his eye
the high wide sky.

A Marriage

The first retainer
he gave to her
was a golden
wedding ring.

The second—late at night
he woke up,
leaned over on an elbow,
and kissed her.

The third and the last—
he died with
and gave up loving
and lived with her.

Ballad of the Despairing Husband

My wife and I lived all alone,
contention was our only bone.
I fought with her, she fought with me,
and things went on right merrily.

But now I live here by myself
with hardly a damn thing on the shelf,
and pass my days with little cheer
since I have parted from my dear.

Oh come home soon, I write to her.
Go fuck yourself, is her answer.
Now what is that, for Christian word?
I hope she feeds on dried goose turd.

But still I love her, yes I do.
I love her and the children too.
I only think it fit that she
should quickly come right back to me.

Ah no, she says, and she is tough,
and smacks me down with her rebuff.
Ah no, she says, I will not come
after the bloody things you've done.

Oh wife, oh wife—I tell you true,
I never loved no one but you.
I never will, it cannot be
another woman is for me.

That may be right, she will say then,
but as for me, there's other men.
And I will tell you I propose
to catch them firmly by the nose.

And I will wear what dresses I choose!
And I will dance, and what's to lose!
I'm free of you, you little prick,
and I'm the one can make it stick.

Was this the darling I did love?
Was this that mercy from above
did open violets in the spring—
and made my own worn self to sing?

She was. I know. And she is still,
and if I love her? then so I will.
And I will tell her, and tell her right . . .

Oh lovely lady, morning or evening or afternoon.
Oh lovely lady, eating with or without a spoon.
Oh most lovely lady, whether dressed or
  ↳ undressed or partly.
Oh most lovely lady, getting up or going to bed
  ↳ or sitting only.

Oh loveliest of ladies, than whom none is more
↳ fair, more gracious, more beautiful.
Oh loveliest of ladies, whether you are just or
↳ unjust, merciful, indifferent, or cruel.
Oh most loveliest of ladies, doing whatever,
↳ seeing whatever, being whatever.
Oh most loveliest of ladies, in rain, in shine, in
↳ any weather.

Oh lady, grant me time,
please, to finish my rhyme.

If You

If you were going to get a pet
what kind of animal would you get.

A soft bodied dog, a hen—
feathers and fur to begin it again.

When the sun goes down and it gets dark
I saw an animal in a park.

Bring it home, to give it to you.
I have seen animals break in two.

You were hoping for something soft
and loyal and clean and wondrously careful—

a form of otherwise vicious habit
can have long ears and be called a rabbit.

Dead. Died. Will die. Want.
Morning, midnight. I asked you

if you were going to get a pet
what kind of animal would you get.

The Tunnel

Tonight, nothing is long enough—
time isn't.
Were there a fire,
it would burn now.

Were there a heaven,
I would have gone long ago.
I think that light
is the final image.

But time reoccurs,
love—and an echo.
A time passes
love in the dark.

The Names

When they came near,
the one, two, three, four,
all five of us sat
in the broken seat.

Oh glad to see,
oh glad to be,
where company
is so derived
from sticks and stones,
bottles and bones.

A Gift of Great Value

Oh that horse I see so high
when the world shrinks into its
relationships, my mother
sees as well as I.

She was born, but I bore with her.
This horse was a mighty occasion!
The intensity of its feet! The height
of its immense body!

Now then in wonder at evening, at
the last small entrance of the night,
my mother calls it, and I
call it *my father*.

With angry face, with no
rights, with impetuosity and
sterile vision—and a great
wind we ride.

Somewhere

The galloping collection of boards
are the house which I afforded
one evening to walk into
just as the night came down.

Dark inside, the candle
lit of its own free will, the attic
groaned then, the stairs
led me up into the air.

From outside, it must have seemed
a wonder that it was
the inside *he* as *me* saw
in the dark there.

Entre Nous

If I can't hope then to hell with it.
I don't want to live like this?

Like this, he said. Where were you?
She was around in back of the bureau

where he pushed her?
Hell no, she just fell.

The Flower

I think I grow tensions
like flowers
in a wood where
nobody goes.

Each wound is perfect,
encloses itself in a tiny
imperceptible blossom,
making pain.

Pain is a flower like that one,
like this one,
like that one,
like this one.

The Door

for Robert Duncan

It is hard going to the door
cut so small in the wall where
the vision which echoes loneliness
brings a scent of wild flowers in a wood.

What I understood, I understand.
My mind is sometime torment,
sometimes good and filled with livelihood,
and feels the ground.

But I see the door,
and knew the wall, and wanted the wood,
and would get there if I could
with my feet and hands and mind.

Lady, do not banish me
for digressions. My nature
is a quagmire of unresolved
confessions. Lady, I follow.

I walked away from myself,
I left the room, I found the garden,
I knew the woman
in it, together we lay down.

Dead night remembers. In December
we change, not multiplied but dispersed,
sneaked out of childhood,
the ritual of dismemberment.

Mighty magic is a mother,
in her there is another issue
of fixture, repeated form, the race renewal,
the charge of the command.

The garden echoes across the room.
It is fixed in the wall like a mirror
that faces a window behind you
and reflects the shadows.

May I go now?
Am I allowed to bow myself down
in the ridiculous posture of renewal,
of the insistence of which I am the virtue?

Nothing for You is untoward.
Inside You would also be tall,
more tall, more beautiful.
Come toward me from the wall, I want to be with You.

So I screamed to You,
who hears as the wind, and changes
multiply, invariably,
changes in the mind.

Running to the door, I ran down
as a clock runs down. Walked backwards,
stumbled, sat down
hard on the floor near the wall.

Where were You.
How absurd, how vicious.
There is nothing to do but get up.
My knees were iron, I rusted in worship, of You.

For that one sings, one
writes the spring poem, one goes on walking.
The Lady has always moved to the next town
and you stumble on after Her.

The door in the wall leads to the garden
where in the sunlight sit
the Graces in long Victorian dresses,
of which my grandmother had spoken.

History sings in their faces.
They are young, they are obtainable,
and you follow after them also
in the service of God and Truth.

But the Lady is indefinable,
she will be the door in the wall
to the garden in sunlight.
I will go on talking forever.

I will never get there.
Oh Lady, remember me
who in Your service grows older
not wiser, no more than before.

How can I die alone.
Where will I be then who am now alone,
what groans so pathetically
in this room where I am alone?

I will go to the garden.
I will be a romantic. I will sell
myself in hell,
in heaven also I will be.

In my mind I see the door,
I see the sunlight before me across the floor
beckon to me, as the Lady's skirt
moves small beyond it.

The Hill

It is some time since I have been
to what it was had once turned me backwards,
and made my head into
a cruel instrument.

It is simple
to confess. Then done,
to walk away, walk away,
to come again.

But that form, I must answer,
is dead in me, completely,
and I will not allow it
to reappear—

Saith perversity, the willful,
the magnanimous cruelty,
which is in me
like a hill.

Kore

As I was walking
   I came upon
chance walking
   the same road upon.

As I sat down
   by chance to move
later
   if and as I might,

light the wood was,
   light and green,
and what I saw
   before I had not seen.

It was a lady
   accompanied
by goat men
   leading her.

Her hair held earth.
   Her eyes were dark.
A double flute
   made her move.

"O love,
   where are you
leading
   me now?"

The Rain

All night the sound had
come back again,
and again falls
this quiet, persistent rain.

What am I to myself
that must be remembered,
insisted upon
so often? Is it

that never the ease,
even the hardness,
of rain falling
will have for me

something other than this,
something not so insistent—
am I to be locked in this
final uneasiness.

Love, if you love me,
lie next to me.
Be for me, like rain,
the getting out

of the tiredness, the fatuousness, the semi-
lust of intentional indifference.
Be wet
with a decent happiness.

Midnight

When the rain stops
and the cat drops
out of the tree
to walk

away, when the rain stops,
when the others come home, when
the phone stops,
the drip of water, the

potential of a caller
any Sunday afternoon.

The Bird

What did you say to me
    that I had not heard.
She said she saw
    a small bird.

Where was it.
    In a tree.
Ah, he said, I thought
    you spoke to me.

Jack's Blues

I'm going to roll up
a monkey and smoke it, put
an elephant in the pot. I'm going out
and never come back.

What's better than that.
Lying on your back, flat
on your back with your
eyes to the view.

Oh the view is blue, I saw that
too, yesterday and you,
red eyes and blue,
funked.

I'm going to roll up
a rug and smoke it, put
the car in the garage and I'm
gone, like a sad old candle.

The Sign Board

The quieter the people are
the slower the time passes

until there is a solitary man
sitting in the figure of silence.

Then scream at him,
come here you idiot it's going to go off.

A face that is no face
but the features, of a face, pasted

on a face until that face
is faceless, answers by

a being nothing there
where there was a man.

The Rescue

The man sits in a timelessness
with the horse under him in time
to a movement of legs and hooves
upon a timeless sand.

Distance comes in from the foreground
present in the picture as time
he reads outward from
and comes from that beginning.

A wind blows in
and out and all about the man
as the horse ran
and runs to come in time.

A house is burning in the sand.
A man and horse are burning.
The wind is burning.
They are running to arrive.

The End of the Day

Oh who is
so cosy with
despair and
all, they will

not come,
rejuvenated, to
the last spectacle
of the day. Look!

the sun is
sinking, now
it's
gone. Night,

good and sweet
night, good
night, good, good
night, has come.

The House

for Louis Zukofsky

Mud put
upon mud,
lifted
to make room,

house
a cave,
and
colder night.

To sleep
in, live in,
to come in
from heat,

all form derived
from kind,
built
with that in mind.

The Pool

My embarrassment at his nakedness,
at the pool's edge,
and my wife, with his,
standing, watching—

this was a freedom
not given me who am
more naked,
less contained

by my own white flesh
and the ability
to take quietly
what comes to me.

The sense of myself
separate, grew
a white mirror
in the quiet water

he breaks with his hands
and feet, kicking,
pulls up to land
on the edge by the feet

of these women
who must know
that for each
man is a speech

describes him, makes
the day grow white
and sure, a quietness of water
in the mind,

lets hang, descriptive
as a risk, something
for which he cannot find
a means or time.

Mind's Heart

Mind's heart, it must
be that some
truth lies locked
in you.

Or else, lies, all
lies, and no man
true enough to know
the difference.

The Name

Be natural,
wise
as you can be,
my daughter,

let my name
be in you flesh
I gave you
in the act of

loving your mother,
all your days
her ways,
the woman in you

brought from
sensuality's measure,
no other,
there was no thought

of it but such
pleasure all women
must be in her,
as you. But not wiser,

not more of nature
than her hair,
the eyes
she gives you.

There will not be another
woman such as you
are. Remember
your mother,

the way you came,
the days of waiting.
Be natural,
daughter, wise

as you can be,
all my daughters,
be women
for men

when that time comes.
Let the rhetoric
stay with me
your father. Let

me talk about it,
saving you such
vicious self-
exposure, let you

pass it on
in you. I cannot
be more than the man
who watches.

Love Comes Quietly

Love comes quietly,
finally, drops
about me, on me,
in the old ways.

What did I know
thinking myself
able to go
alone all the way.

For Love

for Bobbie

Yesterday I wanted to
speak of it, that sense above
the others to me
important because all

that I know derives
from what it teaches me.
Today, what is it that
is finally so helpless,

different, despairs of its own
statement, wants to
turn away, endlessly
to turn away.

If the moon did not . . .
no, if you did not
I wouldn't either, but
what would I not

do, what prevention, what
thing so quickly stopped.
That is love yesterday
or tomorrow, not

now. Can I eat
what you give me. I
have not earned it. Must
I think of everything

as earned. Now love also
becomes a reward so
remote from me I have
only made it with my mind.

Here is tedium,
despair, a painful
sense of isolation and
whimsical if pompous

self-regard. But that image
is only of the mind's
vague structure, vague to me
because it is my own.

Love, what do I think
to say. I cannot say it.
What have you become to ask,
what have I made you into,

companion, good company,
crossed legs with skirt, or
soft body under
the bones of the bed.

Nothing says anything
but that which it wishes
would come true, fears
what else might happen in

some other place, some
other time not this one.
A voice in my place, an
echo of that only in yours.

Let me stumble into
not the confession but
the obsession I begin with
now. For you

also (also)
some time beyond place, or
place beyond time, no
mind left to

say anything at all,
that face gone, now.
Into the company of love
it all returns.

The Rhythm

It is all a rhythm,
from the shutting
door, to the window
opening,

the seasons, the sun's
light, the moon,
the oceans, the
growing of things,

the mind in men
personal, recurring
in them again,
thinking the end

is not the end, the
time returning,
themselves dead but
someone else coming.

If in death I am dead,
then in life also
dying, dying . . .
And the women cry and die.

The little children
grow only to old men.
The grass dries,
the force goes.

But is met by another
returning, oh not mine,
not mine, and
in turn dies.

The rhythm which projects
from itself continuity
bending all to its force
from window to door,
from ceiling to floor,
light at the opening,
dark at the closing.

Water

The sun's
sky in
form of
blue sky
that

water will
never make
even
in
reflection.

Sing, song,
mind's form
feeling
if
mistaken,

shaken,
broken water's
forms, love's
error
in water.

For W.C.W.

The rhyme is after
all the repeated
insistence.

There, you say, and
there, and there,
and *and* becomes

just so. And
what one wants is
what one wants,

yet complexly
as you
say.

Let's
let it go.
I want—

Then there is—
and,
I want.

For No Clear Reason

I dreamt last night
the fright was over, that
the dust came, and then water,
and women and men, together
again, and all was quiet
in the dim moon's light.

A paean of such patience—
laughing, laughing at me,
and the days extend over
the earth's great cover,
grass, trees, and flower-
ing season, for no clear reason.

Something

I approach with such
a careful tremor, always
I feel the finally foolish

question of how it is,
then, supposed to be felt,
and by whom. I remember

once in a rented room on
27th street, the woman I loved
then, literally, after we

had made love on the large
bed sitting across from
a basin with two faucets, she

had to pee but was nervous,
embarrassed I suppose I
would watch her who had but

a moment ago been completely
open to me, naked, on
the same bed. Squatting, her

head reflected in the mirror,
the hair dark there, the
full of her face, the shoulders,

sat spread-legged, turned on
one faucet and shyly pissed. What
love might learn from such a sight.

The Language

Locate *I*
love you some-
where in

teeth and
eyes, bite
it but

take care not
to hurt, you
want so

much so
little. Words
say everything.

I
love you
again,

then what
is emptiness
for. To

fill, fill.
I heard words
and words full

of holes
aching. Speech
is a mouth.

The Window

Position is where you
put it, where it is,
did you, for example, that

large tank there, silvered,
with the white church along-
side, lift

all that, to what
purpose? How
heavy the slow

world is with
everything put
in place. Some

man walks by, a
car beside him on
the dropped

road, a leaf of
yellow color is
going to

fall. It
all drops into
place. My

face is heavy
with the sight. I can
feel my eye breaking.

There Is

There is
as we go we
see there
is a hairy
hole there is
a darkness ex-
panded by
there is a
sense of some
imminence imman-
ence there is
a subject placed
by the verb a
conjunction coord-
inate lines
a graph of indeterminate
feelings there is
sorry for itself
lonely generally
unhappy in its
circumstances.

Anger

1

The time is.
The air seems a cover,
the room is quiet.

She moves, she
had moved. He
heard her.

The children
sleep, the dog fed,
the house around them

is open, descriptive,
a truck through the walls,
lights bright there,

glaring, the sudden
roar of its motor, all
familiar impact

as it passed
so close. He
hated it.

But what does she answer.
She moves
away from it.

In all they save,
in the way of his saving
the clutter, the accumulation

of the expected disorder—
as if each dirtiness,
each blot, blurred

happily, gave
purpose, happily—
she is not enough there.

He is angry. His
face grows—as if
a moon rose

of black light,
convulsively darkening,
as if life were black.

It is black.
It is an open
hole of horror, of

nothing as if not
enough there is
nothing. A pit—

which he recognizes,
familiar, sees
the use in, a hole

for anger and
fills it
with himself,

yet watches on
the edge of it,
as if she were

not to be pulled in,
a hand could
stop him. Then

as the shouting
grows and grows
louder and louder

with spaces
of the same open
silence, the darkness,

in and out, him-
self between them,
stands empty and

holding out his
hands to both,
now screaming

it cannot be
the same, she
waits in the one

while the other
moans in the hole
in the floor, in the wall.

2

Is there some odor
which is anger,

a face
which is rage.

I think I think
but find myself in it.

The pattern
is only resemblance.

I cannot see myself
but as what I see, an

object but a man,
with lust for forgiveness,

raging, from that vantage,
secure in the purpose,

double, split.
Is it merely intention,

a sign quickly adapted,
shifted to make

a horrible place
for self-satisfaction.

I rage.
I rage, I rage.

3

You did it,
and didn't want to,

and it was simple.
You were not involved,

even if your head was cut off,
or each finger

twisted
from its shape until it broke,

and you screamed too
with the other, in pleasure.

4

Face me,
in the dark,
my face. See me.

It is the cry
I hear all
my life, my own

voice, my
eye locked in
self sight, not

the world what
ever it is
but the close

breathing beside
me I reach out
for, feel as

warmth in
my hands then
returned. The rage

is what I
want, what
I cannot give

to myself, of
myself, in
the world.

5

After, what
is it—as if
the sun had

been wrong to return,
again. It was
another life, a

day, some
time gone, it
was done.

But also
the pleasure, the
opening

relief
even in what
was so hated.

6

All you say you want
to do to yourself you do
to someone else as yourself

and we sit between you
waiting for whatever will
be at last the real end of you.

Some Place

I resolved it, I
found in my life a
center and secured it.

It is the house,
trees beyond, a term
of view encasing it.

The weather
reaches only as some
wind, a little

deadened sighing. And
if the life weren't?
when was something to

happen, had I secured
that—had I, *had*
I, insistent.

There is nothing I am,
nothing not. A place
between, I am. I am

more than thought, less
than thought. A house
with winds, but a distance

—something loose in the wind,
feeling weather as that life,
walks toward the lights he left.

Song

I wouldn't
embarrass you
ever.

If there were
not place
or time for it,

I would go,
go elsewhere,
remembering.

I would
sit in a
flower, a face, not

to embarrass
you, would
be unhappy

quietly, would
never
make a noise.

Simpler,
simpler you
deal with me.

The Answer

Will we speak to each other
making the grass bend as if
a wind were before us, will our

way be as graceful, as
substantial as the movement
of something moving so gently.

We break things in pieces like
walls we break ourselves into
hearing them fall just to hear it.

Some Echoes

Some echoes,
little pieces,
falling, a dust,

sunlight, by
the window, in
the eyes. Your

hair as
you brush
it, the light

behind
the eyes,
what is left of it.

Words

You are always
with me,
there is never
a separate

place. But if
in the twisted
place I
cannot speak,

not indulgence
or fear only,
but a tongue
rotten with what

it tastes— There is
a memory
of water, of
food, when hungry.

Some day
will not be
this one, then
to say

words like a
clear, fine
ash sifts,
like dust,

from nowhere.

They

I wondered what had
happened to the chords.
There was a music,

they were following
a pattern. It was
an intention perhaps.

No field
but they walk
in it. No place

without them, any
discretion is useless.
They want a time, they

have a time, each
one in his place, an
endless arrival.

A Sight

Quicker
than that, can't
get off "the
dead center of"

myself. *He/I*
were walking. Then
the place *is/was*
not ever enough. But

the house, if
admitted, were
a curiously wrought
complexity of flesh.

The eyes
windows, the head
roof form with
stubbornly placed

bricks of chimney.
I can remember, I
can. Then when
she first touched me,

when we were
lying in that bed,
was the feeling of
falling into no

matter we both lay
quiet, where
was it. I
felt her flesh

enclose mine. *Cock,*
they say, *prick, dick,*
I put it in her,
I lay there.

Come back, breasts,
come. Back. The sudden
thing of being
no one. I

never felt guilty,
I was confused but
could not feel
wrong, about it.

I wanted to kill her.
I tried it, tentatively,
just a little
hurt. Hurt me.

So immense she was.
All the day
lying flat, lying it seemed
upon a salty sea, the houses

bobbing
around her, under
her, I hung on
for dear life to her.

But when
now I walk, when
the day comes
to trees and a road,

where
is she. Oh, on my
hands and knees, crawl-
ing forward.

A Picture

A little
house with
small
windows,

a gentle
fall of the
ground to
a small

stream. The trees
are both close
and green, a tall
sense of enclosure.

There is a sky
of blue
and a faint sun
through clouds.

A Piece

One and
one, two,
three.

Intervals

Who
am I—
identity
singing.

Place
a lake
on ground, water
finds a form.

Smoke
on the air
goes higher
to fade.

Sun bright,
trees dark green,
a little movement
in the leaves.

Birds singing
measure distance,
intervals between
echo silence.

A Tally

A tally of forces, consequent
memories, of times and places—
habits of preparation at other
points of time and place.

And the hand found the fingers
still on it, moved the thumb,
easily, to the forefinger,
still worked. What

has come. Age? But,
to know itself, needs
occasion, as, no longer young
wants a measure.

The mirror the mind is,
reflective, in that guise,
long habit of much delaying thought
to savor terms of the impression—

it's not as bad as one thought,
but that is relative. Not as simple
as the boat is leaking, he, she, it,
they—or we, you and I, are sinking.

Within the world, this one, many quirks
accomplished, effected, in the thought,
I don't know how, I only live here,
with the body I walk in.

Hence I love you, I did, do,
a moment ago it was daylight,
now dark I wonder what the memory means,
loving you more than I had thought to.

No agreement to stay, see it out,
the dereliction of fleshy duties—
but not burn down the house
for whatever rage was once.

"Oh my love . . ."

Oh my love,
in other times
the things we are
were beauty too.

In ways that were
I never knew
were possible
might talk to you.

Or on and on
and up and down
seasons and days
might make a place

unlike such
awkwardness makes
this one awkward
fall apart.

"As real as thinking . . ."

As real as thinking
wonders created
by the possibility—

forms. A period
at the end of a sentence
which .

began *it was*
into a present,
a presence

saying
something
as it goes.

    .

No forms less
than activity.

All words—
days—or
eyes—

or happening
is an event only
for the observer?

No one
there. Everyone
here.

    •

Small facts
of eyes, hair
blonde, face

looking like a
flat painted
board. How

opaque as if
a reflection
merely, skin

vague glove of
randomly seen
colors.

    •

Inside
and out

impossible
locations—

reaching in
from out-

side, out
from in-

side—as
middle:

one
hand.

The Finger

Either in or out of
the mind, a conception
overrides it. *So that*
that time I was a stranger,

bearded, with clothes that were
old and torn. I was told,
it was known to me, my
fate would be timeless. Again

and again I was to
get it right, the story I
myself knew only the way of,
but the purpose if it

had one, was not mine.
The quiet shatter of the light,
the image folded into
endlessly opening patterns—

had they faced me into
the light so that my
eye was blinded? At moments
I knew they had gone but

searched for her face, the pureness
of its beauty, the endlessly sensual—
but no sense as that now reports it.
Rather, she was beauty, that

Aphrodite I had known of,
and caught sight of as *maid*—
a girlish openness—or known
as a woman turned from the light.

I knew, however, the other,
perhaps even more. She was there
in the room's corner, as she would be,
bent by a wind it seemed

would never stop blowing,
braced like a seabird,
with those endlessly clear grey eyes.
Name her, Athena—what name.

The osprey, the sea, the waves.
To go on telling the story,
to go on though no one hears it,
to the end of my days?

Mercury, Hermes, in dark glasses.
Talk to him—but as if
one talked to the telephone,
telling it to please listen—

is that right, have I said it—
and the reflecting face echoes
some cast of words in mind's eye,
attention a whip of surmise.

And the power to tell
is glory. One unto one
unto one. And though all
mistake it, it is one.

I saw the stones thrown
at her. I felt a radiance transform
my hands and my face.
I blessed her, I was one.

Are there other times?
Is she that woman,
or this one. Am I the man—
and what transforms.

Sit by the fire.
I'll dance a jig I learned
long before we were born
for you and you only then.

I was not to go
as if to somewhere,
was not in the mind
as thinking knows it,

but danced in a jigging
intensive circle
before the fire and its heat
and that woman lounging.

How had she turned herself?
She was largely warm—
flesh heavy—and smiled
in some deepening knowledge.

There are charms.
The pedlar and the small dog
following and the whistled,
insistent song.

I had the pack,
the tattered clothing,
was neither a man nor not one,
all that—

and who was she,
with the fire behind her,
in the mess of that place,
the dust, the scattered pieces,

her skin so warm,
so massive, so stolid in her
smiling the charm did not
move her but rather

kept her half-sleepy attention,
yawning, indulging the manny
who jiggled a world before her
made of his mind.

She was young,
she was old,
she was small.
She was tall with

extraordinary grace. Her face
was all distance, her eyes
the depth of all one had thought of,
again and again and again.

To approach, to hold her,
was not possible.
She laughed and turned
and the heavy folds of cloth

parted. The nakedness
burned. Her heavy breath,
her ugliness, her lust—
but her laughing, her low

chuckling laugh, the way
she moved her hand to the
naked breast, then to
her belly, her hand with its fingers.

Then *shone* —
and whatever is said
in the world, or forgotten,
or not said, makes a form.

The choice is simply,
I will—as mind is a finger,
pointing, as wonder
a place to be.

Listen to me, let
me touch you
there. You are young again,
and you are looking at me.

Was there ever
such foolishness more
than what thinks it knows
and cannot see, was there ever

more? Was the truth
behind us, or before?
Was it one
or two, and who was I?

She was laughing, she was
laughing, at me,
and I danced, and
I danced.

Lovely, lovely woman, let
me sing, *one to*
one to one, and let
me follow.

The Moon

Earlier in the evening the moon
was clear to the east,
over the snow of the yard
and fields—a lovely

bright clarity and perfect
roundness, isolate,
riding as they say the
black sky. Then we went

about our businesses of the
evening, eating supper, talking,
watching television, then
going to bed, making love,

and then to sleep. But before
we did I asked her to look
out the window at the moon
now straight up, so that

she bent her head and looked
sharply up, to see it.
Through the night it must
have shone on, in that

fact of things—another
moon, another night—a
full moon in the winter's
space, a white loneliness.

I came awake to the blue
white light in the darkness,
and felt as if someone
were there, waiting, alone.

Numbers

for Robert Indiana

ONE

What
singular upright flourishing
condition . . .
it enters here,
it returns here.

•

Who was I that
thought it was
another one by
itself divided or multiplied
produces one.

•

This time, this
place, this
one.

•

You are not
me, nor I you.

•

All ways.

•

As of a stick,
stone, some-

thing so
fixed it has

a head, walks,
talks, leads

a life.

TWO
When they were
first made, all the
earth must have
been their reflected
bodies, for a moment—
a flood of seeming
bent for a moment back
to the water's glimmering—
how lovely they came.

              .

What you wanted
I felt, or felt I felt.
This was more than one.

              .

This point of so-called
consciousness is forever
a word making up
this world of more
or less than it is.

    •

Don't leave me.
Love me. One by one.

    •

As if to sit
by me were another
who did sit. So

to make you
mine, in the mind,
to know you.

THREE

They come now with
one in the middle—
either side thus
another. Do they

know who each other
is or simply walk
with this pivot between them.
Here forms have possibility.

    •

When either this
or that becomes
choice, this fact

of things enters.
What had been
agreed now

alters to
two and one,
all ways.

.

The first
triangle, of form,
of people,

sounded a
lonely occasion I
think—the

circle begins
here, intangible—
yet a birth.

FOUR

This number for me
is comfort, a secure
fact of things. The

table stands on
all fours. The dog
walks comfortably,

and two by two
is not an army
but friends who love

one another. Four
is a square,
or peaceful circle,

celebrating return,
reunion,
love's triumph.

    ·

The card which is the
four of hearts must
mean enduring experience
of life. What other
meaning could it have.

    ·

Is a door
four—but
who enters.

    ·

Abstract—yes, as
two and two
things, four things—
one and three.

FIVE

Two by
two with
now another

in the middle
or else at
the side.

        .

From each
of the four
corners draw

a line to
the alternate
points. Where

these intersect
will be
five.

        .

When younger this was
a number used to
count with, and

to imagine a useful
group. Somehow the extra
one—what is more than four—

reassured me there would be
enough. Twos and threes or
one and four is plenty.

        •

A way to draw stars.

SIX
Twisting
        as forms of it
two and three—

        on the sixth
day had finished
        all creation—

hence holy—
        or that the sun
is "furthest from

equator & appears
to pause, before
        returning . . .''

or that it ''contains
        the first even number
(2), and the first odd

        number (3), the former representing
the male member, and the latter
        the *muliebris pudenda* . . .''

Or two triangles interlocked.

SEVEN

We are seven, echoes in
my head like a nightmare of
responsibility—seven
days in the week, seven
years for the itch of
unequivocal involvement.

        •

Look
at
the
light
of
this
hour.

I was born at seven in
the morning and my
father had a monument
of stone, a pillar, put
at the entrance of the
hospital, of which he was head.

   .

*At sixes
and sevens*—the pen
lost, the paper:

a night's dead
drunkenness. Why
the death of something now

so near if *this*
number is holy.
Are all

numbers one?
Is counting forever
beginning again.

   .

Let this be the end of the seven.

EIGHT

Say "eight"—
be patient.

Two fours
show the way.

.

Only this number
marks the cycle—

the eight year interval—
for that confluence

makes the full moon shine
on the longest

or shortest
day of the year.

.

Now summer fades.
August its month—
this interval.

.

She is eight
years old, holds
a kitten, and
looks out at me.

•

Where are you.
One table.
One chair.

•

In light lines count the interval.
Eight makes the time wait quietly.

•

No going back—
though half is
four and
half again
is two.

•

Oct-
ag-
on-
al.

NINE

There is no point
of rest here.
It wavers,

it reflects multiply
the *three*
times three.

Like a mirror
it returns here
by being there.

.

Perhaps in the
emphasis implicit—
over and over—

"triad of triads,"
"triply sacred and perfect
number"—that

resolves what—
in the shifting,
fading containment?

.

Somehow the game
where a nutshell covers
the one object, a

stone or coin, and
the hand is
quicker than the eye—

how is that *nine*,
and not *three*
chances, except that

three imaginations of it
might be, and there are
two who play—

making six, but
the world is real also,
in itself.

    •

More. The nine months
of waiting that discover
life or death—

another life or death—
not yours, not
mine, as we watch.

    •

The serial diminish-
ment or progression of
the products which

helped me remember:
nine times two is one-eight
            nine times nine is eight-one—
at each end,

move forward, backward,
then, and the same
numbers will occur.

        •

What law
or
mystery

is involved
protects
itself.

ZERO

Where are you—who
        by not being here
are here, but here
        by not being here?

There is no trick to reality—
        a mind
makes it, any
        mind. You

147

walk the years in a
        nothing, a no
place I know as well as
        the last breath

I took, blowing the smoke
        out of a mouth
will also go nowhere,
        having found its way.

        •

Reading that primitive systems
seem to have natural cause for
the return to one, after ten—
but this is *not* ten—out of
nothing, one, to return to that—
Americans have a funny way—
somebody wrote a poem about it—
of "doing nothing"—What else
should, *can*, they do?

        •

What
by being not
is—is not
by being.

When holes taste good
we'll put them in our bread

THE FOOL

"With light step, as if earth and its trammels
had little power to restrain him, a young man in
gorgeous vestments pauses at the brink of a
precipice among the great heights of the world;
he surveys the blue distance before him—its
expanse of sky rather than the prospect below.
His act of eager walking is still indicated, though
he is stationary at the given moment; his dog is
still bounding. The edge which opens on the
depth has no terror; it is as if angels were
waiting to uphold him, if it came about that he
leaped from the height. His countenance is full
of intelligence and expectant dream. He has a
rose in one hand and in the other a costly wand,
from which depends over his right shoulder a
wallet curiously embroidered. He is a prince
of the other world on his travels through this
one—all amidst the morning glory, in the keen
air. The sun, which shines behind him, knows
whence he came, whither he is going, and
how he will return by another path after many
days . . ."

Names

Harry has written
all he knows.
Miriam tells
her thought, Peter
says again
his mind. Robert and John,
William, Tom,
and Helen, Ethel,
that woman whose name
he can't remember
or she even him
says to tell
all they know.

America

America, you ode for reality!
Give back the people you took.

Let the sun shine again
on the four corners of the world

you thought of first but do not
own, or keep like a convenience.

People are your own word, you
invented that locus and term.

Here, you said and say, is
where we are. Give back

what we are, these people you made,
us, and nowhere but you to be.

Mazatlán: Sea

The sea flat out,
the light far out,
sky red, the
blobs of dark clouds
seem closer, beyond
the far lateral of
extended sea.

.

Shimmer of reflected
sand tones, the flat
ripples as the water
moves back—an oscil-
lation, endlessly in-
stinct movement—leaves
a ribbing after itself
it then returns to.

.

Bird flicker, light
sharp, flat—the
green hills of the two
islands make a familiar
measure, momently seen.

.

The air is thick
and wet and
comfortably encloses
with the sea's sounds.

.

Sleep—it washes
away.

KIDS WALKING beach,
minnow pools—
who knows which.

.

Nothing grand—
The scale is neither
big nor small.

.

Want to get the sense of "I" into Zukofsky's
"eye"—a locus of experience, not a presumption
of expected value.

.

Here now—
begin!

BOBBIE

Crazy kid-face
skun, in water—
wide hips. The white,
white skin—a big
eared almost feral
toothed woman—
lovely in all particulars.

        •

Other way—dark
eyed, the face a
glow of some other
experience, deepens
in the air.

AGH—MAN
thinks.

        •

Moving away in time,
as they say: *days
later*. Later than this—
what swings in the day's
particulars, one to one.

      •

An unexamined hump
at first of no
interest lifting out
of the beach at
last devoured us all.

      •

Sell the motherfucker for
several hundred dollars.

      •

". . . I ran out of my cabin, both glad and
frightened, shouting, 'A noble earthquake! A
noble earthquake!' feeling sure I was going to
learn something." [John Muir, *The Yosemite*,
p. 59.]

THE KICK
of the foot against . . .

      •

Make time
of irritations,
looking for the
recurrence—

waiting, waiting,
on the edge of its
to be there
where it was, waiting.

　　•

Moving in the mind's
patterns, recognized
because there is where
they happen.

　　•

Grease
on the hands—

Four

Before I die.
Before I die.
Before I die.
Before I die.

How that fact of
seeing someone you love away
from you in time will
disappear in time, too.

.

Here is all there is,
but *there* seems so
insistently across the way.

.

Heal it, be
patient with
it—be quiet.

.

Across the
table,
years.

Here

Past time—those
memories opened
places and minds,
things of such reassurance—

now the twist,
and what was a road
turns to a circle
with nothing behind.

⋅

I didn't know what I could do.
I have never known it
but in doing found it
as best I could.

Here I am still,
waiting for that discovery.
What morning, what way now,
will be its token.

⋅

They all walk by
on the beach,
large, or little,
crippled, on the face
of the earth.

⋅

The wind holds
my leg like

a warm hand.

SOME NIGHTS, a fearful
waking—beside me
you were sleeping,
what your body was

a quiet, apparent
containment. All the world is
this tension, you or me,
seen in that mirror,

patent, pathetic, insured.
I grow bored with lives
of such orders—my own
the least if even yours the most.

.

No one lives in
the life of another—
no one knows.

In the singular
the many cohere,
but not to know it.

Here, *here*, the body
screaming its orders,
learns of its own.

.

What would you have
of the princess—
large ears, to hear?
Hands with soft fingers?

You will ride away
into the forest, you will
meet her there
but you will know her.

Why not another
not expected, some
lovely presence suddenly
declared?

All in your mind
the body is, and of
the body such
you make her.

        •

One, two,
is the rule—

from there to three
simple enough.

Now four
makes the door

back again
to one and one.

     •

My plan is
these little boxes
make sequences . . .

     •

Lift me
from such I
makes such declaration.

     •

Hearing it—*snivelling*—
wanting the reassurance of
another's decision.

There is no one precedes—
look ahead—and behind
you have only where you were.

YOU SEE the jerked
movement, in the
rigid frame, the
boy—the tense stricken

animal, and behind,
the sea moves and
relaxes. The island sits
in its immovable comfort.

What, in the head, goes wrong—
the circuit suddenly
charged with contraries,
and time only is left.

.

The sun drops. The swimmers
grow black in the silver
glitter. The water slurs
and recurs. The air is soft.

COULD WRITE of fucking—
rather its instant or the slow
longing at times of its approach—

how the young man desires,
how, older, it is never known
but, familiar, comes to be so.

How your breasts, love,
fall in a rhythm also familiar,
neither tired nor so young they

push forward. I hate the metaphors.
I want you. I am still alone,
but want you with me.

Listless,
the heat rises—
the whole beach

vacant,
sluggish.
The forms shift

before we know,
before we thought
to know it.

The mind
again, the manner
of mind in the

body, the
weather, the waves,
the sun grows lower

in the faded
sky. Washed
out—the afternoon

of another day
with other people,
looking out of other eyes.

Only the
children, the sea,
the slight wind move

with the
same insistent
particularity.

•

I was sleeping
and saw the context
of people, dense
around me, talked
into their forms, almost

strident. There were
bright colors, intense
voices. We were, like
they say, discussing

some point of procedure—
would they go, or
come—and waking,
no one but my wife there,
the room faint, bare.

•

"It's strange. It's
all fallen
to grey."

.

How much
money is
there now?

Count it
again. There's
enough.

.

What changes.
Is the weather
all there is.

SUCH STRANGENESS of mind I know
I cannot find there more
than what I know.

I am tired of purposes,
intent that leads itself
back to its own belief. I want

nothing more of such brilliance
but what makes the shadows darker
and that fire grow dimmer.

.

Counting age as form
I feel the mark of one
who has been born and grown
to a little past return.

The body will not go
apart from itself to be
another possibility.
It lives where it finds home.

Thinking to alter all
I looked first to myself,
but have learned the foolishness
that wants an altered form.

Here now I am at best,
or what I think I am
must follow as the rest
and live the best it can.

.

There was no one there.
Rather I thought I saw her,
and named her beauty.

For that time we lived
all in my mind
with what time gives.

The substance of one
is not two. No thought
can ever come to that.

I could fashion another
were I to lose her.
Such is thought.

•

Why the echo of
the old music
haunting all? Why

the lift and fall
of the old rhythms,
and aches and pains.

Why one, why two,
why not go utterly
away from all of it.

•

Last night's dream of a complex of people, almost suburban it seemed, with plots to uncover like a thriller. One moment as we walk to some house through the dark, a man suddenly appears behind us who throws himself at us, arms reaching out, but falls short and lands, skids, spread-eagled on the sidewalk. Then later, in another dream, we are bringing beer somewhere on a sort of truck, rather the cab of one, nothing back of it, and I am hanging on the side which I realize is little more than a scaffolding—and the wheels nearly brush me in turning. Then, much later, I hear our dog yelp—three times it now seems—so vividly I'm awake and thinking he must be outside the door of this room though he is literally in another country. Reading Yeats: "May we not learn some day to rewrite our histories, when they touch upon these things?"

WHEN HE and I,
after drinking and
talking, approached
the goddess or woman

become her, and by my
insistence entered
her, and in the ease
and delight of the

168

meeting I was given that
sight gave me myself,
this was the mystery
I had come to—all

manner of men, a
throng, and bodies of
women, writhing, and
a great though seemingly

silent sound—and when
I left the room to them,
I felt, as though hearing
laughter, my own heart lighten.

   •

What do you do,
what do you say,
what do you think,
what do you know.

In London
for Bettina

Homage to Bly & Lorca

_____

"I'm going home to Boston
by God"

•

Signs

____

(red)

EXIT
EXIT
EXIT
EXIT

•

(Cards)

Question—
where do you get a pencil.
Answer.

_____

•

(for Jim Dine)

most common simple
address words everything
in one clear call to me.

.

("Small Dreams")

Scaffolding comes up the side of the building,
pipes, men putting them there. Faces, in, past
one block of windows, then as I'm up in the
bathroom, they appear there too.

.

Ted
is ready.
The bell
rings.

.

Small dreams of home.
Small of home dreams.
Dreams of small home.
Home small dreams of.

.

I love you happily
ever after.

.

(Homesick, etc.)

There is a land
far, far away
and I will go there
every day.

    •

12:30 (<u>Read as Twelve Thirty</u>)

(Berrigan
Sleeps on)

    •

Voices on the phone, over it—wires? Pulsations.
Lovely one of young woman. Very soft and
pleasant. Thinking of Chamberlain and Ultra
Violet—"talking the night away." Fuck
MacCluhan—or how the hell you spell it—and/
or teetering fall, the teething ring, "The Mother
of Us All"—*for Bob*. Call me up. "Don't Bring
Me Down . . ."

    •

Variance of emotional occasion in English
voices—for myself, American, etc. Therefore
awkward at times "to know where one is." In

contrast to Val's Welsh accent—the congruence
with one's own, Massachusetts. Not that they
"sound alike"—but somehow do agree.

.

"London
Postal Area
A-D"

.

Posterior possibilities—
Fuck 'em.

.

"It's 2 hrs. 19 mins. from London
in the train to beautiful country."

"EAT ME"
The favorite delicious dates.

.

Girls
Girls
Girls
Girls

2 X 2

.

Some guy now here inside wandering around
with ladder and bucket. Meanwhile the scaffold-
ing being built outside goes on and on, more
secure.

•

Like German's poem I once translated, something
about "when I kissed you, a beam came through
the room. When I picked you flowers, they took
the whole house away." Sort of an ultimate
hard-luck story.

•

Lovely roofs outside.
Some of the best roofs in London.

•

Surrounded
by bad art.

•

I get
a lot
of writing
done—

"You Americans."

•

H— will pirate primary edition of Wms' *Spring and All*, i.e., it's all there. Check for Whitman's *An American Primer*—long time out of print. Wish he'd reprint as Chas apparently suggests Gorki's *Reminiscences of Tolstoi* [now learn it's been in paperback for some years]. Wish I were home at this precise moment—the sun coming in those windows. The sounds of the house, birds too. Wish I were in bed with Bobbie, just waking up.

•

Wish I were an apple seed
and had John what's-his-name
to plant me.

•

Her strict eye,
her lovely voice.

•

Così fan tutte.
So machin's alle.

•

Wigmore
dry gin
kid.

•

Wish Joan Baez was here
singing "Tears of Rage" in my ear.

Wish I was Bob Dylan—
he's got a subtle mind.

    •

I keep coming—
I keep combing my hair.

    •

Peter Grimes
Disraeli Gears

    •

That tidy habit of sound
relations—must be in the
very works,* like.

_____

*Words work
the author of many pieces

    •

Wish could snap pix in
mind forever of roofs out
window. Print on endurable paper, etc.

    •

With delight he realized
his shirts would last him.

·

I'll get home in 'em.

·

The song of such energy
invites me. The song

of

"The day was gathered on waking . . ."

The day was gathered on waking
into a misty greyness. All the air
was muffled with it, the colors
faded. Not simply then alone—

the house despite its size is full
with us—but an insistent restless
sense of nowhere enough to be
despite the family, the fact of us.

What does one want—more, what
do I say I want. Words give
me sense of something. Days I find
had use for me, how else one thought.

But the nagging, the dripping
weather . . . All the accumulation,
boxes of things piled up the grey
seems to cover, all the insistent junk.

One comes to a place he had not thought to,
looks ahead to whatever,
feels nothing lost but himself.

"Do you think . . ."

Do you think that if
you once do what you want
to do you will want not to do it.

Do you think that if
there's an apple on the table
and somebody eats it, it
won't be there anymore.

Do you think that if
two people are in love with one another,
one or the other has got to be
less in love than the other at
some point in the otherwise happy relationship.

Do you think that if
you once take a breath, you're by
that committed to taking the next one
and so on until the very process of
breathing's an endlessly expanding need
almost of its own necessity forever.

Do you think that if
no one knows then whatever
it is, no one will know and
that will be the case, like
they say, for an indefinite
period of time if such time
can have a qualification of such time.

Do you know anyone,
really. Have you been, really,
much alone. Are you lonely,
now, for example. Does anything
really matter to you, really, or
has anything mattered. Does each
thing tend to be there, and then not
to be there, just as if that were it.

Do you think that if
I said, *I love you,* or anyone
said it, or you did. Do you
think that if you had all
such decisions to make and could
make them. Do you think that
if you did. That you really
would have to think it all into
reality, that world, each time, new.

People

for Arthur Okamura

I knew where they were,
in the woods. My sister
made them little houses.

Possibly she was one,
or had been one
before. They were there,

very small but quick,
if I moved. I
never saw them.

How big is small. What
are we in. Do
these forms of us take shape, then.

Stan told us of the shape
a march makes, in
anger, a sort of small

head, the vanguard, then
a thin neck, and then,
following out, a kind of billowing,

loosely gathered *body*, always
the same. It must be
people seen from above

have forms, take place,
make an insistent pattern,
not suburbs, but the way

they gather in public places,
or, hidden from others,
look one by one, must be

there to see, a record if
nothing more. "In a tree
one may observe the hierarchies

of monkeys," someone says. "On
the higher branches, etc." But
not like that, no, the kids

run, watch the *wave* of them
pass. See the form of their
movement pass, like the wind's.

I love you, I thought,
suddenly. My hands
are talking again. In-

side each finger must
be several men. They
want to talk to me.

On the floor the dog's eye
reflects the world, the people
passing there, before him.

The car holds possibly
six people, comfortably,
though each is many more.

I'll never die or else will
be the myriad people all
were always and must be—

in a flower, in a
hand, in some
passing wind.

    •

These things
seen from inside, human,
a head, hands

and feet. I can't
begin again to make
more than was made.

You'll see them
as flowers, called
the flower people—

others as rocks,
or silt, some
crystalline or even

a stream of smoke.
Why here at all
—the first question—

no one easily answers,
but they've taken place
over all else. They live

now in everything, as everything.
I keep hearing
their voices, most happily

laughing, but the screaming
is there also. Watch
how they go together.

They are not isolated
but meld into continuous
place, one to one, never alone.

     .

From whatever place
they may have come from,
from under rocks,

that moistness, or the sea,
or else in those
slanting places of darkness,

in the woods, they
are here and ourselves
with them. All

the forms we know,
the designs, the
closed-eye visions of

order—these too they are,
in the skin we
share with them.

If you twist one
even insignificant part
of your body

to another, imagined
situation of where it
might be, you'll

feel the pain of all
such distortion and
the voices will

flood your head with
terror. No thing
you can do can

be otherwise than
these *people*, large
or small, however

you choose to think
them—a drop of
water, glistening

on a grassblade, or
the whole continent,
the whole world of *size*.

    •

Some stories begin,
when I was young—
this also. It tells

a truth of things,
of people. There used
to be so many, so

big one's eyes went
up them, like a ladder,
crouched in a wall.

Now grown large, I
sometimes stumble, walk
with no knowledge of

what's under foot.

    •

Some small
echo
at the earth's edge

recalls
these voices,
these small

persistent
movements,
these people,

the circles,
the holes they
made, the

one
multiphasic
direction,

the going,
the coming,
the lives.

I
fails in
the forms

of them, I
want
to go home.

Massachusetts

What gentle echoes,
half heard sounds
there are around here.

    .

You place yourself in
such relation, you hear
everything that's said.

Take it or leave it.
Return it to a particular
condition.

Think
slowly. See
the things around you,

taking place.

    .

I began wanting a sense
of melody, e.g., following
the tune, became somehow
an image, then several,
and I was watching those things
becoming in front of me.

    .

The *you* imagined locates
the response. Like turning
a tv dial. The message,
as one says, is information,
a form of energy. The wisdom
of the ages is "electrical" impulse.

.

Lap of water
to the hand, lifting
up, slaps
the side of the dock—

Darkening air, heavy
feeling in the air.

.

A PLAN

On some summer day
when we are far away
and there is impulse and time,
we will talk about all this.

Rain

Things one sees through
a blurred sheet of glass,
that figures, predestined,
conditions of thought.

.

Things seen through
plastic, rain sheets,
trees blowing in a blurred
steady sheet of vision.

.

Raining, trees blow,
limbs flutter, leaves
wet with the insistent
rain, all over, everywhere.

.

Harry will write
Mabel on Monday.
The communication
of human desires

flows in an apparently
clear pattern, aftersight,
now they know
for sure what it was.

If it rains, the woods
will not be so dry
and danger averted,
sleep invited.

Rain (2)

Thoughtful of you, I was
anticipating change in
the usual manner. If the rain

made the day unexpected,
in it I took a place.
But the edge of the room

now blurred, or the window
did, or you, sitting, had
nonetheless moved away.

Why is it an empty house
one moves through, shouting
these names of people there?

The Temper

The temper is fragile
as apparently it wants to be,
wind on the ocean, trees
moving in wind and rain.

Kitchen

The light in the morning
comes in the front windows,
leaving a lace-like pattern
on the table and floor.

•

In the silence now
of this high square room
the clock's tick adjacent
seems to mark old time.

•

Perpetually sweeping
this room, I want it
to be like it was.

Here

Here is
where there
is.

Echo

Broken heart, you
timeless wonder.

What a small
place to be.

True, true
to life, to life.

In the Fall

The money is cheap
in the fall
by the river
in the woods.

Hanging leaves
hang on, red, yellow,
the wind is sharp,
distances increase.

Still

Still the same
day?
Tomorrow.

Home

Patsy's
brother
Bill—

Meg's
mother—
Father's

home.
Sweet
home.

One Day

One day after another—
perfect.
They all fit.

Place

There was a path
through the field
down to the river,

from the house
a walk of
a half an hour.

Like that—
walking,
still,

to go swimming,
but only
if somone's there.

Flesh

Awful rushes at times
floating out in that emptiness
don't answer nothing for no one.

Seeing dear flesh float by—
days emptied of sun and wind,
hold on to trees and dirt.

Want it under me, body,
want legs to keep working—
don't think anymore of it.

You face passes down the street—
you hair that was so lovely,
your body, won't wait for me.

Oh Mabel

Oh Mabel, we
will never walk
again the streets

we walked in
1884, my love,
my love.

For My Mother:
Genevieve Jules Creeley

April 8, 1887–October 7, 1972

Tender, semi-
articulate flickers
of your

presence, all
those years
past

now, eighty-
five, impossible to
count them

one by one, like
addition, sub-
traction, missing

not one. The last
curled up, in
on yourself,

position you take
in the bed, hair
wisped up

on your head, a
top knot, body
skeletal, eyes

closed against,
it must be,
further disturbance—

breathing a skim
of time, lightly
kicks the intervals—

days, days and
years of it,
work, changes,

sweet flesh caught
at the edges,
dignity's faded

dilemma. It
is *your* life, oh
no one's

forgotten anything
ever. They want
to make you

happy when
they remember. Walk
a little, get

up, now, die
safely,
easily, into

singleness, too
tired with it
to keep

on and on.
Waves break at
the darkness

under the road, sounds
in the faint
night's softness. Look

at them, catching
the light, white
edge as they turn—

always again
and again. Dead
one, two,

three hours—
all these minutes
pass. Is it,

was it, ever
you alone
again, how

long you kept
at it, your
pride, your

lovely, confusing
discretion. Mother, I
love you—for

whatever that
means,
meant—more

than I know, body
gave me my
own, generous,

inexorable place
of you. I feel
the mouth's sluggish-

ness, slips on
turns of things
said, to you,

too soon, too late,
wants to
go back to beginning,

smells of the hospital
room, the doctor
she responds

to now, the
order—get me
there. "Death's

let you out—"
comes true,
this, that,

endlessly circular
life, and we
came back

to see you one
last
time, this

time? Your head
shuddered,
it seemed, your

eyes wanted,
I thought,
to see

who it was.
I am here,
and will follow.

Sitting Here

for Kate

Roof's peak is eye,
sky's grey, tree's
a stack of lines,

wires across it. This
is window, this is
sitting at the table,

thinking of you,
far away,
whose face is

by the mirror on the bureau.
I love you, I said,
because I wanted to,

because I know you,
my daughter, my
daughter.

I don't want you
to walk away. I
get scared

in this loneliness.
Be *me* again
being born, be the little

wise one walks
quietly by, in the sun,
smiles silently,

grows taller and taller.
Because all these things
passing, changing,

all the things
coming and going
inside, outside—

I can't hold them,
I want to but
keep on losing them.

As if to catch your hand, then,
your fingers, to hang on,
as if to feel

it's all right here
and will be, that
world *is* wonder,

being simply beyond us,
patience its savor,
and to keep moving,

we love what we love,
what we have,
what we have to.

I don't know—
this fact of time spinning,
days, weeks, months, years,

stuffed in some attic.
Or—where can we run,
why do I want to?

As if that touch of you
had, unknowing,
turned me around again

truly to face you,
and your face is wet,
blurred, with tears—

or is it simply years later,
sitting here, and whatever
we were has gone.

Up in the Air

Trees
breathing
air.

•

No longer
closely here
no longer.

•

Fire still burning
in heart. People
move in the oak brush.
Day widens,
music in the room.
Think it's back
where you left it?
Think, think
of nothing.

•

Mind tremors,
(taught) taut rubber,
shimmers of bounce.

•

Sensual body,
a taut skin?

Not the same
mistake "twice"?

Reechoes, re-
collects.

   •

Each one
its own imagination

"at best"

This
can be thought of?

of

   •

Tree tops
your head

   •

"That's very frequent in French."

   •

Indignity
no name

   •

Those old hotels.

•

"I'm going to take a trip
in that old gospel ship

"I'm going far beyond the sky

—"bid this world goodbye"

"I can scarcely wait . . .
I'll spend my time in prayer—"

"And go sailing through
                    the air . . ."

*If you are ashamed of me,
you ought not to be . . .*

You will sure be left behind,
while *I'm* sailing through

                    the air . . .

        •

Beauty's desire shall be endless
and a hell of a lot of fun.

        •

Luck?
Looks like.

        •

Falls
always.

.

You go
that way.
I'll
go this.

.

Many times broke
but never poor.
Many times poor
but never broke.

.

Be welcome
to it.

.

Mind-
ful of feeling,

thinking it.

.

Sun's hand's shadow.
Air passes. Friends.

.

The right one.
The wrong one.
The other one.

·

Heavy time moves
imponderably present.

·

Let her
sing it
for herself.

·

Keep a distance
recovers space.

"River wandering down . . ."

River wandering down
below in the widening green
fields between the hills—
and the sea and the town.

Time settled, or waiting,
or about to be. People,
the old couple, the two babies,
beside me—the so-called

aeroplane. Now
be born,
be born.

So There

for Penelope

Da. Da. Da da.
Where is the song.
What's wrong
with life

ever. More?
Or less—
days, nights,
these

days. *What's gone
is gone forever
every time*, old friend's
voice here. I want

to stay, somehow,
if I could—
if I would? Where else
to go.

The sea here's out
the window, old
switcher's house, vertical,
railroad blues, *lonesome*

whistle, etc. Can you
think of Yee's Cafe
in Needles, California
opposite the train

station—can you keep
it ever
together, old buddy, talking
to yourself again?

Meantime some *yuk*
in Hamilton has blown
the whistle on a charming
evening I wanted

to remember otherwise—
the river there, that
afternoon, sitting,
friends, wine & chicken,

watching the world go by.
Happiness, happiness—
so simple. What's
that anger is that

competition—sad!—
when this at least
is free,
to put it mildly.

My aunt Bernice
in Nokomis,
Florida's last act,
a poem for Geo. Washington's

birthday. Do you want
to say "it's bad"?
In America, old sport,
we shoot first, talk later,

or just take you out to dinner.
No worries, or not
at the moment,
sitting here eating bread,

cheese, butter, white wine—
like Bolinas, "Whale Town,"
my home, like they say,
in America. It's *one* world,

it can't be another.
So the beauty,
beside me, rises,
looks now out window—

and breath keeps on breathing,
heart's pulled in
a sudden deep, sad
longing, to want

to stay—be another
person some day,
when I grow up.
The world's somehow

forever that way
and its lovely, roily,
shifting shores, sounding now,
in my ears. My ears?

Well, what's on my head
as two skin appendages,
comes with the package.
I don't want to

argue the point.
Tomorrow
it changes, gone,
abstract, new places—

moving on. Is this
some old time weird
Odysseus trip
sans paddle—up

the endless creek?
Thinking of you,
baby, thinking
of all the things

I'd like to say and do.
Old fashioned time
it takes to be
anywhere, at all.

Moving on. Mr. Ocean,
Mr. Sky's
got the biggest blue eyes
in creation—

here comes the sun!
While we can,
let's do it, let's
have fun.

Talking

Faded back last night
into older dreams, some

boyhood lost innocences.
The streets have become inaccessible

and when I think of people,
I am somehow not one of them.

Talking to the doctor-
novelist, he read me a poem

of a man's horror, in Vietnam,
child and wife lost to him—

his own son sat across from me,
about eight, thin, intent—

and myself was like a huge,
fading balloon, that could hear

but not be heard, though we
talked and became clear friends.

I wanted to tell him I was
an honest, caring man. I wanted

the world to be more simple,
for all of us. His wife said,

driving back, that my hotel's bar
was a swinging place in the '50s.

It was a dark, fading night.
She spoke quickly, obliquely,

along for the ride, sitting
in the front seat beside him.

I could have disappeared, gone
away, seen them fading too,

war and peace, death,
life, still no one.

There

Miles back
in the wake,
days faded—

nights sleep seemed
falling down
into some deadness—

killing it,
thinking dullness,
thinking body

was dying.
Then
you changed it.

Myself

What, younger, felt
was possible, now knows
is not—but still
not changed enough—

Walked by the sea,
unchanged in memory—
evening, as clouds
on the far-off rim

of water float,
pictures of time,
smoke, faintness—
still the dream.

I want, if older,
still to know
why, human, men
and women are

so torn, so lost,
why hopes cannot
find better world
than this.

Shelley is dead and gone,
who said,
"Taught them not this—
to know themselves;

their might Could not repress
the mutiny within,
And for the morn
of truth they feigned,

deep night
Caught them ere evening . . ."

This World

If night's the harder,
closer time, days
come. The morning
opens with light

at the window.
Then, as now, sun
climbs in blue sky.
At noon

on the beach
I could watch
these glittering
waves forever,

follow their sound
deep into mind
and echoes—
let light

as air
be relief.
The wind
pulls at face

and hands,
grows cold. What
can one think—
the beach

is myriad stone.
Clouds pass,
grey undersides,
white clusters

of air, all
air. Water
moves at the edges,
blue, green,

white twists
of foam.
What then
will be lost,

recovered.
What
matters as one
in this world?

The House

Mas-Soñer
Restaurat—Any—
1920 . . . Old
slope of roof,

gutted windows,
doors, the walls,
with crumbling stucco
shows the mortar

and stones
underneath. Sit
on stone wall adjacent
topped with brick,

ground roundabout's weeds,
red dirt, bare rock.
Then look east
down through valley—

fruit trees in their rows,
the careful fields,
the tops of the other
farmhouses below—

then the city, in haze,
the sea. Look
back in time
if you can—

think of the
myriad people
contained in this instant
in mind. But the well

top's gone, and debris
litters entrance.
Yet no sadness,
no fears

life's gone out.
Could put it all right,
given time,
and need, and money,

make this place sing,
the rooms open
and warm, and spring
come in at the windows

with the breeze—
the white blossom
of apple
still make this song.

Flaubert's Early Prose

"Eventually he dies
out of a lack of will to live,
out of mere weariness and sadness . . ."

And then he is hit by a truck
on his way home from work,

and/or a boulder
pushed down onto him
by lifelong friends of the family
writes FINIS to his suffering—

Or he goes to college,
gets married,
and *then* he dies!

Or finally he doesn't die at all,
just goes on living,
day after day in the same old way . . .

He is a very interesting man,
this intensively sensitive person,
but he has to die somehow—

so he goes by himself to the beach,
and sits down and thinks,
looking at the water to be found there,

"Why was I born? Why
am I living?"—like
an old song, *cheri*—
and then he dies.

After

I'll not write again
things a young man
thinks, not the words
of that feeling.

There is no world
except felt, no
one there but
must be here also.

If that time was
echoing, a vindication
apparent, if flesh
and bone coincided—

let the body be.
See faces float
over the horizon let
the day end.

Love

There are words voluptuous
as the flesh
in its moisture,
its warmth.

Tangible, they tell
the reassurances,
the comforts,
of being human.

Not to speak them
makes abstract
all desire
and its death at last.

Blues

for Tom Pickard

Old time blues
and things to say—
not going home
till they come to get me.

See the sky
black as night,
drink what's
there to drink.

God's dead,
men take over,
world's round,
all over.

Think of it,
all those years,
no one's the wiser
even older.

Flesh, flesh,
screams in body,
you know,
got to sleep.

Got to eat, baby,
got to.
No way
you won't.

When I lay down
big bed
going to pillow
my sleeping head.

When I fall,
I fall,
straight down
deep I'm going.

No one
touch me
with
their doubting mind.

You don't
love me
like you
say you do, you

don't do me
like you
said
you would.

What I say
to people
don't mean
I don't love,

what I
do don't
do, don't don't
do enough.

Think I drink
this little glass,
sit on my ass,
think about

life, all
those things,
substance.
I could touch you.

Times in jail
I was scared
not of being hurt
but that people lock you up,

what's got to be
cruel is you know,
and I don't, you say
you got the truth.

I wouldn't listen
if I was drunk, couldn't hear
if I was stoned,
you tell me right or don't.

Come on home, brother,
you make a fool,
get in trouble, end up
in jail.

I'm in the jailhouse now.
When they lock the door,
how long is what
you think of.

Believe in what's there,
nowhere else it will be.
They kill you,
they kill me.

Both dead,
we'll rise again.
They believe in Christ,
they'll believe in men.

I Love You

I see you, Aunt Bernice—
and your smile anticipating reality.
I don't care any longer that you're older.
There are times all the time the same.

I'm a young old man here on earth,
sticks, dust, rain, trees, people.
Your cat killing rats in Florida was incredible—
Pete—weird, sweet presence. Strong.

You were good to me. You had *wit*—
value beyond all other human possibility.
You could smile at the kids, the old cars.
Your house in N.H. was lovely.

Four Years Later

When my mother
died, her things were
distributed

so quickly. Nothing
harsh about it,
just gone,

it seemed, but
for small
mementos, pictures

of family, dresses,
a sweater,
clock.

Looking back
now, wish
I'd talked

more to her.
I tried
in the hospital

but our habit
was too deep—
we didn't

speak easily.
Sitting
now, here,

early morning,
by myself,
can hear her—

as "Bob,
do what you have to—
I trust you—"

words like
"presumption," possibly
"discretion"—some

insistent demand to
cover living
with clothes—not

"dressed up" but
common, faithful—
what no other can know.

Later

1

Shan't be winding
back in blue
gone time ridiculous,
nor lonely

anymore. Gone,
gone—wee thin
delights, hands
held me, mouths

winked with white
clean teeth. Those
clothes have fluttered
their last regard

to this passing
person walks by
that flat back-
yard once and for all.

2

You won't want to be early
for passage of grey mist
now rising from the faint

river alongside the childhood
fields. School bell rings,
to bring you all in again.

That's mother sitting there,
a father dead in heaven,
a dog barks, steam of

drying mittens on the stove,
blue hands, two doughnuts
on a plate.

3

The small
spaces of existence,
sudden

smell of burning
leaves makes
place in time

these days
(these days)
passing,

common
to one
and all.

4

Opening
the boxes packed
in the shed,

at the edge
of the porch
was to be

place to sit
in the sun,
glassed over,

in the winter
for looking out
to the west,

see the shadows
in the early
morning lengthen,

sharp cold
dryness of air,
sounds of cars,

dogs, neighbors,
persons
of house, toilet

flush, pan
rattle, door
open, never done.

5

Eloquent,
my heart,

thump bump—
My Funny Valentine

6

If you saw
dog pass, in car—

looking out, possibly
indifferently, at you—

would you—*could* you—
shout, "Hey, Spot!

It's me!" After all
these years,

no dog's coming home
again. Its skin's

moldered
through rain, dirt,

to dust, hair alone
survives, matted tangle.

Your own, changed,
your hair, greyed,

your voice not the one
used to call him home,

"Hey, Spot!" *The world's
greatest dog's* got

lost in the world,
got lost long ago.

7

Oh sadness,
boring

preoccupation—
rain's wet,

clouds
pass.

8

Nothing "late" about the
"no place to go" old folks—

or "hell," or
"Florida this winter."

No "past" to be
inspired by "futures,"

scales of the imperium,
wonders of what's next.

When I was a kid, I
thought like a kid—

I *was* a kid,
you dig it. But

a hundred and fifty years later,
that's a whole long time to

wait for the train.
No doubt West Acton

was improved by the discontinuance
of service, the depot taken down,

the hangers-around there moved
at least back a street to Mac's Garage.

And you'll have to drive your own car
to get to Boston—or take the bus.

These days, call it "last Tuesday,"
1887, my mother was born,

and now, sad to say,
she's dead. And especially "you"

can't argue
with the facts.

9

Sitting up here in
newly constituted

attic room 'mid
pipes, scarred walls,

the battered window
adjacent looks out

to street below. It's fall,
sign woven in iron

rails of neighbor's porch:
"Elect Pat Sole."

O sole mio, mother,
thinking of old attic,

West Acton farmhouse,
same treasures here, the boxes,

old carpets, the smell.
On wall facing, in chalk:

KISS ME. *I love you.*
Small world of these pinnacles,

places ride up in these
houses like clouds,

and I've come as far,
as high, as I'll go.

Sweet weather, turn
now of year . . .

The old horse chestnut,
with trunk a stalk like a flower's,

gathers strength to face winter.
The spiked pods of its seeds

start to split, soon will drop.
The patience, of small lawns, small hedges,

papers blown by the wind,
the light fading, gives way

to the season. School's
started again. Footsteps fall

on sidewalk down three
stories. It's man-made

endurance I'm after,
it's love for the wear

and the tear here,
goes under, gets broken, but stays.

Where finally else
in the world come to rest—

by a brook, by a
view with a farm

like a dream—in
a forest? In a house

has walls all around it?
There's more always here

than just me, in this room,
this attic, apartment,

this house, this world,
can't escape.

10

In testament
to a willingness

to *live*, I,
Robert Creeley,

being of sound body
and mind, admit

to other preoccupations—
with the future, with

the past. But now—
but now the wonder of life is

that *it is* at all,
this sticky sentimental

warm enclosure,
feels place in the physical

with others,
lets mind wander

to wondering thought,
then lets go of itself,

finds a home
on earth.

For Rene Ricard

Remote control factors
of existence, like
"I wanted it this way!"

And hence to Lenox
one summer's day
with old friend, Warren Tallman,

past charming hills
and valleys give class
to that part of western Mass.

I can get funny—
and I can get lost,
go wandering on,

with friends like signboards
flashing past
in those dark nights of the soul.

All one world, Rene,
no matter one's half
of all it is or was.

So walking with you and Pepi,
talking, gossiping,
thank god—the useful news—

what's presently the word
of X, Y, and Z
in NYC, the breezes

on the hill, by the orchard
where Neil sits under tree,
blow the words away,

while he watches me talk,
mouth poems for them,
though he can't hear a word.

This is art,
the public act
that all those dirt roads lead to,

all those fucking bogs
and blown out tires
and broken fan belts—

willed decision—
call it,
though one's too dumb to know.

For me—and possibly
for only me—a bird
sits in a lousy tree,

and sings and sings
all goddamn day,
and what I do

is write it down,
in words
they call them:

him, and *it*, and *her*,
some story this
will sometimes tell

or not. The bird
can't care, the
tree can hardly hold it up—

and me is least of all
its worry. What then
is this life all about.

Simple. It's garbage
dumped in street,
a friend's quick care,

someone who hates you
and won't go way,
a breeze

blowing past Neil's
malfunctioning dear ears,
a blown-out dusty room,

an empty echoing kitchen,
a physical heart
which goes or stops.

For you—
because you carry wit with you,
and you are there somehow

at the hard real times,
and you know them too—
a necessary love.

Desultory Days

for Peter Warshall

Desultory days,
time's wandering
impermanences—

like, *what's for lunch*,
Mabel? Hunks
of unwilling

meat got chopped
from recalcitrant
beasts? "No tears

for this vision"—
nor huge strawberries
zapped from forlorn Texas,

too soon, too soon . . .
We will meet again
one day, we will

gather at the river
(Paterson perchance)
so turgidly oozes by,

etc. Nothing new in the world
but us, the human
parasite eats up

that self-defined reality
we talked about in
ages past. Now prophecy declares,

got to get on with it,
back to the farm, else die
in streets inhuman

'spite we made them every one.
Ah friends, before I die,
I want to sit awhile

upon this old world's knee,
yon charming hill, you see,
and dig the ambient breezes,

make of life
such gentle passing pleasure!
Were it then wrong

to avoid, as might be said,
the heaped-up canyons of the dead—
L.A.'s drear smut, and N.Y.C.'s

crunched millions? I don't know.
It seems to me
what can salvation be

for less than 1%
of so-called population
is somehow latent fascism

of the soul. What leaves behind
those other people,
like they say,

reneges on Walter Whitman's
19th century Mr. Goodheart's
Lazy Days and Ways In Which

we might still *save the world*.
I loved it but
I never could believe it—

rather, the existential
terror of New England
countrywoman, Ms.

Dickinson: "The Brain, within its Groove
Runs evenly—and true—
But let a Splinter swerve—

" 'Twere easier for You—//
To put a Current back—
When Floods have slit the Hills—

"And scooped a Turnpike for Themselves—
And Trodden out the Mills—"
moves me. My mind

to me a nightmare is—
that thought of days,
years, went its apparent way

without itself, with
no other company than thought.
So—*born to die*—why

take everything with us?
Why the meagerness
of life deliberately,

why the patience
when of no use,
and the anger, when it is?

I am no longer
one man—
but an old one

who is human again
after a long time,
feels the meat contract,

or stretch, upon bones,
hates to be alone
but can't stand interruption.

Funny
how it all works out,
and Asia is

after all *how much money
it costs*—
either to buy or to sell it.

Didn't they have a
world too? But then
they don't look like us,

do they? But they'll get us,
someone will—they'll find us,
they won't leave us here

just to die
by ourselves
all alone?

If I Had My Way

If I had my way, dear,
all these fears, these insistent
blurs of discontent would fade,

and there be
old time meadows
with brown and white cows,

and those boulders,
still in mind, marked
the solid world. I'd

show you these ridiculous,
simple happinesses, the wonders
I've kept hold on

to steady the world—
the brook, the woods,
the paths, the clouds, the house

I lived in,
with the big barn
with my father's sign on it:

FOUR WINDS FARM.
What life ever is
stays in them.

You're young, like
they say. Your life
still comes to find

me—my honor
its choice. Here is the place
we live in

day by day, to learn
love, having it,
to begin again

again. Looking up,
this sweet room
with its colors, its forms,

has become you—
as my own life
finds its way

to you also,
wants to haul
all forward

but learns to let go,
lets the presence
of you be.

If I had my way, dear,
forever there'd be
a garden of roses—

on the old player piano
was in the sitting room
you've never seen nor will now see,

nor my mother or father,
or all that came after,
was a life lived,

all the labor, the pain?
the deaths, the wars,
the births

of my children? On
and on then—
for you and for me.

Prayer to Hermes

for Rafael López-Pedraza

Hermes, god
of crossed sticks,
crossed existence,
protect these feet

I offer. Imagination
is the wonder
of the real, and I am
sore afflicted with

the devil's doubles,
the twos, of this
half-life,
this twilight.

Neither one nor two
but a mixture
walks here
in me—

feels forward,
finds behind
the track, yet
cannot stand

still or be here
elemental, be more
or less a man,
a woman.

What I understand
of this life,
what was right
in it, what was wrong,

I have forgotten
in these days
of physical change.
I see the ways

of knowing, of
securing, life grow
ridiculous. A weakness,
a tormenting, relieving weakness

comes to me. My hand
I see at arm's end—
five fingers, fist—
is not mine?

Then must I forever
walk on, *walk on*—
as I have and
as I can?

Neither truth, nor love,
nor body itself—
nor anyone of any—
become me?

Yet questions
are tricks,
for me—
and always will be.

This moment the grey,
suffusing fog
floats in the quiet courtyard
beyond the window—

this morning grows now
to noon, and somewhere above
the sun warms the air
and wetness drips as ever

under the grey, diffusing
clouds. This weather,
this winter, comes closer.
This—*physical* sentence.

I give all
to you, hold
nothing back,
have no strength to.

My luck
is your gift,
my melodious
breath, my stumbling,

my twisted commitment,
my vagrant
drunkenness, my confused
flesh and blood.

All who know me
say, *why* this man's
persistent pain, the scarifying
openness he makes do with?

Agh! brother spirit,
what do they know
of whatever *is* the instant
cannot wait a minute—

will find heaven in hell,
will be there again even now,
and *will* tell of itself
all, *all* the world.

The Edge

Long over whatever edge,
backward a false distance,
here and now, sentiment—

to begin again, forfeit
in whatever sense an end,
to give up thought of it—

hanging on to the weather's edge,
hope, a sufficiency, thinking
of love's accident, this

long way come with no purpose,
face again, changing,
these hands, feet, beyond me,

coming home, an intersection,
crossing of one and many,
having all, having nothing—

Feeling thought, heart, head
generalities, all abstract—
no place for me or mine—

I take the world and lose it,
miss it, misplace it,
put it back or try to, can't

find it, fool it, even feel it.
The snow from a high sky,
grey, floats down to me softly.

This must be the edge
of being before the thought of it
blurs it, can only try to recall it.

Song

Love has no other friends
than those given it, as us,
in confusion of trust and dependence.

We want the world a wonder
and wait for it to become one
out of our simple bodies and minds.

No doubt one day it will
still all come true as people
do flock to it still until

I wonder where they'll all find room
to honor love in their own turn
before they must move on.

It's said the night comes
and ends all delusions and dreams,
in despite of our present sleeping.

But here I lie with you
and want for nothing more
than time in which to—

till love itself dies with me,
at last the end I thought to see
of everything that can be.

No! All vanity, all mind flies
but love remains, love, nor dies
even without me. Never dies.

Time

for Willy

Out window roof's slope
of overlapped cedar shingles
drips at its edges, morning's still

overcast, grey, Sunday—
goddamn the god that will not
come to his people in their want,

serves as excuse for death—
these days, far away, blurred world
I had never believed enough.

For this wry, small, vulnerable
particular child, my son—
my dearest and only William—

I want a human world, a
chance. Is it my age
that fears, falters in some faith?

These ripples of sound, poor
useless prides of mind,
name the things, the feelings?

When I was young,
the freshness of a single
moment came to me

with all hope, all tangent wonder.
Now I am one, inexorably
in this body, in this time.

All generality? There is
no one here but words,
no thing but echoes.

Then by what imagined right
would one force another's life
to serve as one's own instance,

his significance be mine—
wanting to sing, come
only to this whining sickness . . .

Up from oneself physical
actual limit to lift
thinking to its intent

if such in world there is
now all truth to tell
this child is all it is

or ever was. The place of
time oneself in the net
hanging by hands will

finally lose their hold,
fall. Die. Let this son
live, let him live.

Self-Portrait

He wants to be
a brutal old man,
an aggressive old man,
as dull, as brutal
as the emptiness around him,

He doesn't want compromise,
nor to be ever nice
to anyone. Just mean,
and final in his brutal,
his total, rejection of it all.

He tried the sweet,
the gentle, the "oh,
let's hold hands together"
and it was awful,
dull, brutally inconsequential.

Now he'll stand on
his own dwindling legs.
His arms, his skin,
shrink daily. And
he loves, but hates equally.

Mother's Voice

In these few years
since her death I hear
mother's voice say
under my own, I won't

want any more of that.
My cheekbones resonate
with her emphasis. Nothing
of not wanting only

but the distance there from
common fact of others
frightens me. I look out
at all this demanding world

and try to put it quietly back,
from me, say, thank you,
I've already had some
though I haven't

and would like to
but I've said no, she has,
it's not my own voice anymore.
It's higher as hers was

and accommodates too simply
its frustrations when
I at least think I want more
and must have it.

Versions

after Hardy

Why would she come to him,
come to him,
in such disguise

to look again at him—
look again—
with vacant eyes—

and why the pain still,
the pain—
still useless to them—

as if to begin again—
again begin—
what had never been?

    •

Why be
persistently
hurtful—
no truth
to tell
or wish to?
Why?

    •

The weather's still grey
and the clouds gather
where they once walked
out together,

greeted the world with
a faint happiness,
watched it die
in the same place.

Oh Love

My love is a boat
floating
on the weather, the water.

She is a stone
at the bottom of the ocean.
She is the wind in the trees.

I hold her
in my hand
and cannot lift her,

can do nothing
without her. Oh love,
like nothing else on earth!

The Movie Run Backward

The words will one day come
back to you, birds returning,
the movie run backward.

Nothing so strange in its talk,
just words. The people
who wrote them are the dead ones.

This here paper talks like anything
but is only one thing,
"birds returning."

You can "run the movie
backward" but "the movie run
backward." The movie run backward.

Bresson's Movies

A movie of Robert
Bresson's showed a yacht,
at evening on the Seine,
all its lights on, watched

by two young, seemingly
poor people, on a bridge adjacent,
the classic boy and girl
of the story, any one

one cares to tell. So
years pass, of course, but
I identified with the young,
embittered Frenchman,

knew his almost complacent
anguish and the distance
he felt from his girl.
Yet another film

of Bresson's has the
aging Lancelot with his
awkward armor standing
in a woods, of small trees,

dazed, bleeding, both he
and his horse are,
trying to get back to
the castle, itself of

no great size. It
moved me, that
life was after all
like that. You are

in love. You stand
in the woods, with
a horse, bleeding.
The story is true.

Ambition

Couldn't guess it,
couldn't be it—

wasn't ever
there then. Won't

come back, don't
want it.

Still Too Young

I was talking to older
man on the phone

who's saying something
and something are five

when I think it's four,
and all I'd hoped for

is going up in abstract smoke,
and this call is from California

and selling a house,
in fact, two houses,

is losing me money more
than I can afford to,

and I thought I was winning
but I'm losing again

but I'm too old to do it again
and still too young to die.

Sad Advice

If it isn't fun, don't do it.
You'll have to do enough that isn't.

Such is life, like they say,
no one gets away without paying

and since you don't get to keep it
anyhow, who needs it.

Echoes

Step through the mirror,
faint with the old desire.

Want it again,
never mind who's the friend.

Say yes to the wasted
empty places. The guesses

were as good as any.
No mistakes.

Still Dancers

Set the theme
with a cadence
of love's old
sweet song—

No harm in
the emotional
nor in remembering all
you can or want to.

Let the faint, faded music
pour forth its wonder
and bewitch whom it will,
still dancers under the moon.

All The Way

Dance a little,
don't worry.

There's all the way
till tomorrow

from today
and yesterday.

Simple directions, direction,
to follow.

Beside Her to Lie

He'd like the edge
of her warmth here
"beside her to lie"

in trusting comfort
no longer contests
he loves and wants her.

Rachel Had Said

for R. G.

Rachel had said
the persons of her life
now eighty and more
had let go themselves

into the *larger* life,
let go of it, *them*
were persons personal,
let flow so, flower,

larger, more in it,
the garden, desire,
heaven's imagination
seen in being

here among us every-
where in open
wonder about them, in
pain, in pleasure, blessed.

Oh Max

for Max Finstein

1

Dumbass clunk plane "American
Airlines" (well-named) waits at gate

for hour while friend in Nevada's
burned to ash. The rabbi

won't be back till Sunday.
Business lumbers on

in cheapshit world of
fake commerce, *buy and sell,*

what today, what
tomorrow. Friend's dead—

out of it, won't be back
to pay phoney dues. The best

conman in country's
gone and you're left in

plane's metal tube squeezed out
of people's pockets, pennies

it's made of, *big bucks,*
nickels, dimes all the same.

You won't understand it's forever—
one time, just *one time*

you get to play,
go for broke, *forever*, like

old-time musicians,
Thelonious, Bud Powell, Bird's

horn with the chewed-through reed,
Jamaica Plain in the 40's

—Izzy Ort's, The Savoy. Hi Hat's
now gas station. It goes fast.

Scramble it, make an omelet
out of it, for the hell of it. Eat

these sad pieces. Say it's
paper you wrote the world on

and guy's got gun to your head—
go on, he says, *eat it . . .*

You can't take it back.
It's gone. Max's dead.

2

What's memory's
agency—why so much
matter. Better remember

all one can forever—
never, *never* forget.
We met in Boston,

1947, he was out of jail
and just married, lived
in sort of hotel-like

room off Washington Street,
all the lights on,
a lot of them. I never

got to know her well,
Ina, but his daughter
Rachel I can think of

now, when she was 8,
stayed with us, Placitas, wanted bicycle,
big open-faced kid, loved

Max, her father, who,
in his own fragile way,
was good to her.

In and out
of time, first Boston,
New York later—then

he showed up in N.M.,
as I was leaving, 1956,
had the rent still paid

for three weeks on
"The Rose-Covered Cottage" in Ranchos
(*where sheep ambled o'er bridge*)

so we stayed,
worked the street, like they say,
lived on nothing.

Fast flashes—the women
who love him, Rena, Joyce,
Max, the *mensch*, makes

poverty almost fun,
hangs on edge, keeps traveling.
Israel—they catch him,

he told me, lifting
a bottle of scotch at the airport,
tch, tch, let him stay

(I now think) 'cause
'he wants to.
Lives on kibbutz.

So back to New Mexico,
goyims' Israel sans the plan
save Max's ("Kansas City," "Terre Haute")

New Buffalo (friend told me
he yesterday saw that on bus placard
and thought, that's it! Max's place.)

People and people and people.
Buddy, Wuzza, Si
Perkoff, and Sascha,

Big John C., and Elaine,
the kids. Joel and Gil,
LeRoi, Cubby, back and back

to the curious end
where it bends away into
nowhere or Christmas he's

in the army, has come home,
and father, in old South Station,
turns him in as deserter, ashamed,

ashamed of his son. Or the man
Max then kid with his papers
met nightly at Summer Street

subway entrance and on Xmas
he gives him a dime for a tip . . .
No, old man, your son

was not wrong. "America"
just a vagueness, another place,
works for nothing, gets along . . .

3
In air
there's nowhere
enough not
here, nothing

left to speak
to but you'll
know as plane
begins its

descent, like
they say, it
was the place
where you were,

Santa Fe
(holy fire) with
mountains
of blood.

4

Can't leave, never could,
without more, just
one more

for the road.
Time to go makes
me stay—

Max, *be happy*,
be good, broken
brother, *my man*, useless

words
now
forever.

Heaven Knows

Seemingly never until one's dead
is there possible measure—

but of what then or for what
other than the same plagues

attended the living with misunderstanding
and wanted a compromise as pledge

one could care for any of them
heaven knows, if that's where one goes.

Echo

Back in time
for supper
when the lights

For Ted Berrigan

After, size of place
you'd filled
in suddenly emptied
world all too apparent

and as if New England
shrank, grew physically
smaller like Connecticut,
Vermont—all the little

things otherwise unattended
so made real by you,
things to do today,
left empty, waiting

sadly for no one
will come again now.
It's all moved inside,
all that dear world

in mind for forever,
as long as one walks
and talks here,
thinking of you.

Fathers

Scattered, aslant
faded faces a column
a rise of the packed
peculiar place to a
modest height makes
a view of common lots
in winter then, a ground
of battered snow crusted
at the edges under
it all, there under
my fathers their
faded women, friends,
the family all echoed,
names trees more tangible
physical place more tangible
the air of this place the road
going past to Watertown
or down to my mother's
grave, my father's grave, not
now this resonance of
each other one was his, his
survival only, his curious
reticence, his dead state,
his emptiness, his acerbic
edge cuts the hands to
hold him, hold on, wants
the ground, *wants* this frozen ground.

Memory Gardens

Had gone up to
down or across dis-
placed eagerly
unwitting hoped for

mother's place in time
for supper just
to say anything
to her again one

simple clarity her
unstuck glued
deadness emptied
into vagueness hair

remembered wisp that
smile like half
her eyes brown eyes
her thinning arms

could lift her
in my arms so
hold to her so
take her in my arms.

My Own Stuff

"My own stuff" a
flotsam I could
neither touch quite
nor get hold of, fluff,
as with feathers, milk-
weed, the evasive
lightness distracted yet
insistent to touch
it kept poking, trying
with my stiffened
fingers to get hold of
its substance I had
even made to be
there its only
reality my own.

Funeral

Why was grandma
stacked in sitting room
so's people could come
in, tramp through.

What did we eat
that day before
we all drove off
to the cemetery in Natick

to bury her with grandpa
back where the small air-
port plane flew over
their modest lot there

where us kids could
look through the bushes,
see plane flying around or
sitting on the ground.

Supper

Time's more than
twilight mother at
the kitchen table over
meal the boiled potatoes
Theresa's cooked with meat.

Mother's Photograph

Could you see present
sad investment of
person, its clothes,
gloves and hat,

as against yourself
backed to huge pine tree,
lunch box in hand in
homemade dress aged

ten, to go to school
and learn to be somebody,
find the way will
get you out of the

small place of home
and bring them with
you, out of it too,
sit them down in a new house.

A Calendar

THE DOOR (JANUARY)
Hard to begin
always again and again,

open that door
on yet another year

faces two ways
but goes only one.

Promises, promises . . .
What stays true to us

or to the other
here waits for us.

HEARTS (FEBRUARY)
No end to it if
"heart to heart"
is all there is

to buffer, put against
harshness of this weather,
small month's meagerness—

"Hearts are trumps,"
win out again
against all odds,

beat this
drab season of bitter cold
to save a world.

MARCH MOON (MARCH)

Already night and day move
more closely, shyly, under this frozen

white cover, still rigid with
locked, fixed, deadened containment.

The dog lies snuffling, snarling
at the sounds beyond the door.

She hears the night, the new moon,
the white, wan stars, the

emptiness momently will break
itself open, howling, intemperate.

"WHAN THAT APRILLE . . ." (APRIL)

When April with his showers sweet
the drought of March has pierced to the root
and bathed every vein in such liqueur
its virtue thus becomes the flower . . .

When faded harshness moves to be
gone with such bleakness days had been,
sunk under snows had covered them,
week after week no sun to see,

306

then restlessness resolves in rain
after rain comes now to wash all clean
and soften buds begin to spring
from battered branches, patient earth.

Then into all comes life again,
which times before had one thought dead,
and all is outside, nothing in—
and so it once more does begin.

WYATT'S MAY (MAY)

In May my welth and eke my liff, I say,
have stonde so oft in such perplexitie . . .
                        —SIR THOS. WYATT

In England May's mercy
is generous. The mustard

covers fields in broad swaths,
the hedges are white flowered—

but it is meager, so said.
Having tea here, by the river,

huge castle, cathedral, time
passes by in undigested,

fond lumps. Wyatt died
while visiting friends nearby,

307

and is buried in Sherborne Abbey—
"England's first sonnet-maker . . ."

May May reward him and all
he stood for more happily now

because he sang May,
maybe for all of us:

"Arise, I say, do May some obseruance!
Let me in bed lie dreming in mischaunce . . ."

So does May's mind remember all
it thought of once.

SUMMER NIGHTS (JUNE)

Up over the edge of
the hill climbs the
bloody moon and

now it lifts the far
river to its old familiar
tune and the hazy

dreamlike field—and all
is summer quiet, summer
nights' light airy shadow.

"BY THE RUDE BRIDGE . . ." (JULY)

Crazy wheel of days
in the heat, the revolution
spaced to summer's

insistence. That sweat,
the dust, time earlier they
must have walked, run,

all the way from Lexington
to Concord: "By the rude
bridge that arched the flood . . ."

By that enfolding small river
wanders along by grasses'
marge, by thoughtless stones.

VACATION'S END (AUGUST)

Opened door chinks
let sun's restlessness

inside eighth month
going down now

earlier as day begins
later, time running down,

air shifts to edge
of summer's end

and here they've gone,
beach emptying

to birds, clouds,
flash of fish, tidal

waters waiting, shifting,
ripple in slight wind.

HELEN'S HOUSE (SEPTEMBER)

Early morning far trees lift
through mist in faint outline

under sun's first rose,
dawn's opalescence here,

fall's fading rush to color,
chill under the soft air.

Foreground's the planted small fruit trees,
cut lawn, the firs, as now

on tall dying tree beyond
bird suddenly sits on sticklike branch.

Walk off into this weather?
Meld finally in such air?

See goldenrod, marigold, yarrow, tansey
wait for their turn.

OLD DAYS (OCTOBER)

River's old look
from summers ago
we'd come to swim

now yellow, yellow
rustling, flickering
leaves in sun

middle of October
water's up, high sky's blue,
bank's mud's moved,

edge is
closer,
nearer than then.

THE TALLY (NOVEMBER)

Sitting at table
wedged back against wall,

the food goes down in
lumps swallowed

in hunger, in
peculiar friendship

meets rightly again
without reason

more than common bond, the children
or the old cannot reach

for more
for themselves.

We'll wonder,
wander, in November,

count days and ways
to remember, keep away

from the tally,
the accounting.

MEMORY (DECEMBER)

I'd wanted
ease of year,
light in the darkness,
end of fears.

For the babe newborn
was my belief,
in the manger,
in that simple barn.

So since childhood
animals
brought back kindness,
made possible care.

But this world now
with its want, its pain,
its tyrannic confusions
and hopelessness,

sees no star
far shining,
no wonder as light
in the night.

Only us then
remember, discover,
still can care for
the human.

Song

What's in the body you've forgotten
and that you've left alone
and that you don't want—

or what's in the body that you want
and would die for—
and think it's all of it—

if life's a form to be forgotten
once you've gone and no regrets,
no one left in what you were—

That empty place is all there is,
and/if the face's remembered,
or dog barks, cat's to be fed.

Stairway to Heaven

Point of hill
we'd come to, small
rise there, the friends
now separate, cars
back of us by
lane, the stones,
Bowditch, etc., location,
Tulip Path, hard
to find on the
shaft, that insistent
rise to heaven
goes down and down,
with names like floors,
ledges of these echoes,
Charlotte, Sarah,
Thomas, Annie
and all, as with
wave of hand I'd
wanted them one
way or other to
come, go with them.

Tree

for Warren

You tree
of company—

here
shadowed branches,

small,
twisted comfortably

your size,
reddish buds' clusters—

all of
you I love

here
by the simple river.

Broad Bay

Water's a shimmer,
banks green verge,
trees' standing shadowed,
sun's light slants,
gulls settle white
on far river's length.
All is in a windy echo,
time again
    a far sense.

The Company

for the Signet Society, April 11, 1985

Backward—as if retentive.
"The child is father to the man"
or some such echo of device,
a parallel of use and circumstance.

Scale become implication.
Place, postcard determinant—
only because someone sent it.
Relations—best if convenient.

"Out of all this emptiness
something must come . . ." Concomitant
with the insistent banality, small, still
face in mirror looks simply vacant.

Hence blather, disjunct, incessant
indecision, moving along on
road to next town where what waited
was great expectations again, empty plate.

So there they were, expectably ambivalent,
given the Second World War
"to one who has been long in city pent,"
trying to make sense of it.

We—*morituri*—blasted from classic
humanistic *noblesse oblige*, all the garbage
of either so-called side, hung on
to what we thought we had, an existential

raison d'être like a pea
some faded princess tries to sleep on,
and when that was expectably soon gone,
we left. We walked away.

Recorders ages hence will look for us
not only in books, one hopes, nor only under rocks
but in some common places of feeling,
small enough—but isn't the human

just that echoing, resonant edge
of what it knows it knows,
takes heart in remembering
only the good times, yet

can't forget whatever it was,
comes here again, fearing this
is the last day, this is the last,
the last, the last.

Boat

Rock me, boat.
Open, open.

Hold me,
little cupped hand.

Let me come in,
come on

board you, sail
off, *sail off* . . .

The Seasons

"Therefore all seasons will be sweet to thee . . ."
—S. T. COLERIDGE

for Jasper Johns

Was it *thunk* suck
of sound an insistent

outside into the patience
abstract waited was lost

in such simple flesh *où
sont les* mother and

father so tall the green
hills echoed and light

was longer, longer, into
the sun, all the small

body bent at last to
double back into one

and one and one wonder,
paramour pleasure.

    •

High air's lightness heat
haze grasshopper's chirr

sun's up hum two close
wet sweat time's hung in space

dust deep greens a wave of grasses
smells grow faint sounds echo

the hill again up and down
we go—

*summer, summer, and not even
the full of it . . .*

Echoes again body's time a
ticking a faint insistent

intimate skin wants weather
to reassure.

            •

All grown large world
round *ripeness is all*

an orange pumpkin harsh
edge now of frost an

autumnal moon over the
far off field leads back

to the house all's dead
silence the peculiarly

constructed one you were
all by yourself   *Shine on*

Hear the walls of fall
The dark flutes of autumn

sound softly . . . Oh love,
love, remember me.

            •

As if because or
whenever it was it was

there again muffled mute
an extraordinary quiet

white and cold far off
hung in the air without

apparent edge or end
nowhere one was or if

then gone waited
come full circle again

deep and thick and even
again and again

323

having thought to go nowhere
had got there.

·

The seasons, tallies of earth,
keep count of time,
say what it's worth.

Dreams

What you think you
eat at some table like
a pig with people
you don't even

know and lady there
feeds you all and you,
finally you at least
are full, say, look at

them still eating! Why
(says a woman, another
sitting next to me) those
others still eating you

so cannily observed are
unlike you who *could* be fed
because you were hungry! But
them, they can't—they

are possessed by the
idea of hunger, *never* enough
to eat for them, agh . . .
Or you either, dreamer,

who tells this simple
story being all these
same offensive persons
in one empty head.

     ·

In dreams begin the
particulars of those
echoes and edges,

the quaint ledges of
specific childhood nailed
to my knees and

leaning in unison
while the other
men went off, the

women working, the
kids at baleful
play, mud-colored

with rocks and stones and
trees years ago in
Albuquerque, New Mexico we'd

stopped the night I dreamt
I was to be child forever
on way to get the kids from camp.

     ·

326

Have you ever
had vision as if

you were walking
forward to some

edge of water through
the trees, some country

sunlit lane, some
place was just ahead

and opening as your body
elsewise came

and you had
been in two places?

If

Up the edge of the window out to
tree's overhanging branches sky
light on facing building up to
faint wash blue up on feet ache
now old toes wornout joints make
the wings of an angel so I'd fly.

Sparks Street Echo

Flakes falling
out window make
no place, no place—

no faces, traces,
wastes of whatever
wanted to be—

was here
momently, mother,
was here.

Focus

Patches of grey
sky tree's

lines window
frames the

plant hangs
in middle.

Plague

When the world has become a pestilence,
a sullen, inexplicable contagion,

when men, women, children
die in no sense realized, in

no time for anything, a
painful rush inward, isolate—

as when in my childhood the
lonely leper pariahs so seemingly

distant were just down the street,
back of drawn shades, closed doors—

no one talked to them, no one
held them anymore, no one waited

for the next thing to happen—as
we think now the day begins

again, as we look for the faint sun,
as they are still there, we hope, and we are coming.

Age

Most explicit—
the sense of trap

as a narrowing
cone one's got

stuck into and
any movement

forward simply
wedges one more—

but where
or quite when,

even with whom,
since now there is no one

quite with you— Quite? Quiet?
English expression: *Quait?*

Language of singular
impedance? A dance? An

involuntary gesture to
others *not* there? What's

wrong here? How
reach out to the

other side all
others live on as

now you see the
two doctors, behind

you, in mind's eye,
probe into your anus,

or ass, or bottom,
behind you, the roto-

rooter-like device
sees all up, concludes

"like a worn-out inner tube,"
"old," prose prolapsed, person's

problems won't do, must
cut into, cut out . . .

The world is a round but
diminishing ball, a spherical

ice cube, a dusty
joke, a fading,

faint echo of its
former self but remembers,

sometimes, its past, sees
friends, places, reflections,

talks to itself in a fond,
judgemental murmur,

alone at last.
I stood so close

to you I could have
reached out and

touched you just
as you turned

over and began to
snore not unattractively,

no, never less than
attractively, my love,

my love—but in this
curiously glowing dark, this

finite emptiness, *you, you, you*
are crucial, hear the

whimpering back of
the talk, the approaching

fears when I may
cease to be me, all

lost or rather lumped
here in a retrograded,

dislocating, imploding
self, a uselessness

talks, even if finally to no one,
talks and talks.

Consolatio

What's gone is gone.
What's lost is lost.

What's felt as pulse—
what's mind, what's home.

Who's here, where's there—
what's patience now.

What thought of all,
why echo it.

Now to begin—
Why fear the end.

What

What would it be
like walking off
by oneself down

that path in the
classic woods the light
lift of breeze softness

of this early evening and
you want some time
to yourself to think

of it all again
and again an
empty ending?

Life

All the ways to go,
the echoes, made sense.

It was as fast as that,
no time to figure it out.

No simple straight line,
you'd get there in time

enough standing still.
It came to you

whatever you planned to do.
Later, you'd get it together.

Now it was here.
Time to move.

Eight Plus

Inscriptions for Eight Bollards
at 7th & Figueroa, LA

for James Surls

What's still here settles
at the edges of this
simple place still
waiting to be seen.

•

I didn't go
anywhere and
I haven't
come back!

•

You went by so
quickly thinking
there's a whole world
in between.

•

It's not a
final distance,
this here
and now.

•

How much I would
give just to know
you're standing in
whatever way here.

.

Human eyes
are lights to me
sealed
in this stone.

.

No way to
tell you anything
more than
this one.

.

You walk tired
or refreshed, are
past in a moment,
but saw me.

.

Wish happiness
most for us,
whoever we are,
wherever.

.

If I sit here
long enough,
all will pass me by
one way or another.

.

Nothing left out,
it's all in a heap,
all the people
completed.

.

Night's eye is
memory
in day-
light.

.

I've come and gone from here
with no effect,
and now feel
no use left.

.

How far from
where it
was I'll
never know.

.

You there
next to the others
in front of
the one behind!

    •

No one speaks
alone. It
comes out
of something.

    •

Could I think
of all you
must have felt?
Tell me.

    •

What's inside,
what's the place
apart from
this one?

    •

They say this
used to be
a forest
with a lake.

    •

I'm just
a common
rock,
talking.

.

World's
still got
four
corners.

.

What's
that
up there
looking down?

.

You've got a nice
face and
kind eyes and
all the trimmings.

.

We talk like
this too
often someone
will get wise!

"Ever since Hitler . . ."

Ever since Hitler
or well before that
fact of human appetite
addressed with brutal
indifference others
killed or tortured or ate
the same bodies they
themselves had we ourselves
had plunged into density
of selves all seeming stinking
one no possible way
out of it smiled or cried
or tore at it and died
apparently dead at last
just no other way out.

Helsinki Window

for Anselm Hollo

Go out into brightened
space out there the fainter
yellowish place it
makes for eye to enter out
to greyed penumbra all the
way to thoughtful searching
sight of all beyond that
solid red both brick and seeming
metal roof or higher black
beyond the genial slope I
look at daily house top on
my own way up to heaven.

     •

Same roof, light's gone
down back of it, behind
the crying end of day, "I
need something to do," it's
been again those other
things, what's out there,
sodden edge of sea's
bay, city's graveyard, park
deserted, flattened aspect,
leaves gone colored fall
to sidewalk, street, the end
of all these days but
still this regal light.

•

Trees stripped, rather shed
of leaves, the black solid trunks up
to fibrous mesh of smaller
branches, it is weather's window,
weather's particular echo, here
as if this place had been once,
now vacant, a door that had had
hinges swung in air's peculiar
emptiness, greyed, slumped elsewhere,
asphalt blank of sidewalks, line of
linearly absolute black metal fence.

•

Old sky freshened with cloud bulk
slides over frame of window the
shadings of softened greys a light
of air up out of this dense high
structured enclosure of buildings
top or pushed up flat of bricked roof
frame I love *I love* the safety of
small world this door frame back
of me the panes of simple glass yet
airy up sweep of birch trees sit in
flat below all designation declaration
here as clouds move so simply away.

•

Windows now lit close out the
upper dark the night's a face
three eyes far fainter than
the day all faced with light
inside the room makes eye re-
flective see the common world
as one again no outside coming
in no more than walls and post-
card pictures place faces across
that cautious dark the tree no
longer seen more than black edge
close branches somehow still between.

        •

He was at the edge of this
reflective echo the words blown
back in air a bubble of suddenly
apparent person who walked to
sit down by the familiar brook and
thought about his fading life
all "fading life" in tremulous airy
perspect saw it hover in the surface
of that moving darkness at the edge
of sun's passing water's sudden depth
his own hands' knotted surface the
sounding in himself of some other.

        •

One forty five afternoon red
car parked left hand side
of street no distinguishing
feature still wet day a bicycle
across the way a green door-
way with arched upper window
a backyard edge of back wall
to enclosed alley low down small
windows and two other cars green
and blue parked too and miles
and more miles still to go.

.

This early still sunless morning when a chair's
creak translates to cat's cry a blackness still
out the window might be apparent night when the
house still sleeping behind me seems a bag of
immense empty silence and I feel the children
still breathing still shifting their dreams an
enigma will soon arrive here and the loved one
centers all in her heavy sleeping arm out the
leg pushed down bedclothes this body unseen un-
known placed out there in night I can feel all
about me still sitting in this small spare pool of
light watching the letters the words try to speak.

.

Classic emptiness it
sits out there edge of
hierarchic roof top it
marks with acid fine edge
of apparent difference it
is *there* here *here* that
sky so up and out and where
it wants to be no birds no
other thing can for a
moment distract it be
beyond its simple space.

Shadow

There is a shadow
to intention a place
it comes through and
is itself each stasis
of its mindedness ex-
plicit walled into
semblance it is a
seemingly living place
it wants it fades it
comes and goes it puts
a yellow flower in a pot
in a circle and looks.

Chain

Had they told you, you
were "four or more cells
joined end to end," the Latin,
catena, "a chain," the loop,
the running leap to actual
heaven spills at my stunned
feet, pours out the imprison-
ing threads of genesis,
oh light beaded necklace,
chain round my neck, my
inexorably bound birth, the sweet
closed curve of fading life?

Body

Slope of it,
hope of it—
echoes faded,
what waited

up late inside
old desires
saw through
the screwed importunities.

This regret?
Nothing's left.
Skin's old,
story's told—

but still touch,
selfed body,
wants other,
another mother

to him, her
insistent "sin"
he lets in
to hold him.

Selfish bastard,
headless catastrophe.
Sans tits, cunt,
wholly blunt—

fucked it up,
roof top, loving cup,
sweatered room,
old love's tune.

Age dies old,
both men and women cold,
hold at last no one,
die alone.

Body lasts forever,
pointless conduit,
floods in its fever,
so issues others parturient.

Through legs wide,
from common hole site,
aching information's dumb tide
rides to the far side.

INDEX OF TITLES
AND FIRST LINES

Designer:	Barbara Jellow
Compositor:	Wilsted & Taylor
Text:	11/14 Aldus
Display:	Aldus
Printer:	Malloy Lithographing
Binder:	Malloy Lithographing